An Amazing Life

THE EXTRAORDINARY LIFE OF A
FRIEND OF GOD AND HOW YOU
CAN BECOME ONE

BOLA OLIVIA OGEDENGBE

AN AMAZING LIFE
Copyright © 2019 Bola Olivia Ogedengbe
All rights reserved.

No part of this publication may be reproduced, stored in a retrieval system, distributed, or transmitted in any form or by any means, including photocopying, recording, or other electronic or mechanical methods, except for brief quotations in printed reviews, without the prior written permission of the publisher.

All Scripture quotations, unless otherwise indicated, are taken from the New International Version. Used by permission.
Printed in France

ISBN: 9791095039181

First published: December 2019

OTHER BOOKS BY AUTHOR
Reborn, A New Identity
Reborn, 30 day devotional/Workbook
An Eye to the Crown
Le Feu de Dieu
Appelez à l'Existence
An Amazing Life Workbook

Dedication

I wish to honour my leaders and mentors who have shown me the way in ministry and life. They taught and are still teaching me to walk in faith, honour God and live a life of excellence.

TABLE OF CONTENTS

Introduction   1

BOOK ONE - AN EXTRAORDINARY LIFE   9

Preface 11

Access to divine secrets 13

Divine Interaction 21

Favour and influence with God 29

The faithfulness of God - Divine Intervention 37

Epilogue   49

BOOK TWO - BECOMING A FRIEND OF GOD   51

Preface 53

Know Him 55

Trust Him 81

Agree with Him 109

Obey Him 129

Commune with Him 151

Honour Him 171

Epilogue   191

About the Author   193

INTRODUCTION

THERE IS SOMETHING REMARKABLE ABOUT YOUTH - dreams. Given the right conditions, our minds soar to unimaginable heights. We envision great things for which we were made, remarkable things we are meant to achieve. As far back as I can remember I have always had great aspirations. I always felt I was supposed to live for something great. And there were dreams aplenty. But nothing prepared me for the stunning reality of what God had planned for me even before I knew Him. He wanted to make me His friend and does each one of us.

Indeed, an invitation to divine intimacy is an unimagined consequence of faith in Christ. Many come to the Lord in search of divine help. Many come looking for answers to existential questions. Others come in search of love. Friendship with God rarely features on our agenda. However, we heartily rejoice that we now have a friend in Jesus. He is undeniably a true Friend, one who knows us, loves us and understands us. It is an amazing truth, and many of us never go beyond it. Yet, it is only the beginning of something more. And that something is the point of this book. What is a friend?

What is a friend?

Friendship is defined as the state of being friends or of being friendly. A friend is 'one attached to another by affection or esteem[1]'. A friend is one who favours or supports someone or something.

Who is a friend of God?

First and foremost, a friend of God is one whom God sees as His friend, not one who sees God as their friend. What qualifies a human being to be a friend of God? Is it by meeting His needs and by taking care of Him? Is God in need of help as we often are from our friends? No. Rather, it is about holding Him in high esteem and having deep affection for Him. It is about favouring and supporting His cause. A friend of God is one whose life and conduct manifest their regard for Him and their commitment to His Person. He or she is the one who moves the heart of God through their devotion to Him.

God's plan from the beginning

Divine friendship was God's plan from the beginning. The first humans had a close relationship with God. They knew Him, were devoted to Him and communed

---

1   Grove, P. B. (2002). Webster's third new international dictionary of the English language, unabridged: A Merriam-Webster. Springfield, MA: Merriam-Webster.

with Him. Unfortunately, our first parents shunned the relationship. They suspected God of unholy intentions, betrayed Him and lost that friendship. Openness and transparency were replaced by suspicion and subterfuge. Enmity took the place of friendship. This is clear in the Genesis account.

> And they heard the voice of the LORD God walking in the garden in the cool of the day: and Adam and his wife hid themselves from the presence of the LORD God amongst the trees of the garden. And the LORD God called unto Adam, and said unto him, Where art thou? (Genesis 3:8-9).

We know the story. Intimacy and communion with God vanished, men drifted away from God and with each generation sunk deeper into rebellion. Yet men like Abraham and Moses, men like Enoch and Noah stood out among their contemporaries. They connected to the heart of God. Friendship speaks of harmony, agreement and good rapport. These men lived in harmony with God, despite their sometimes gross imperfections and personal failures. They had one quest—a single-minded pursuit of obedience to God's purposes.

One man stands out among all in the biblical account as having received this magnificent testimony from God. God speaks of him as 'my friend'. His name is Abraham. This patriarch was a man who walked with God, albeit imperfectly, as all humans do. We have much to learn from his relationship with God. Referring to him, God says through the prophet Isaiah to the people of Israel:

> But you, Israel, my servant, Jacob, whom I have chosen, you descendants of Abraham my friend... (Isaiah 41:8).

Surely of all the honours a human can receive, of all the awards, titles, degrees, encomiums, none can surpass this one. The apostle James also testifies thus:

> And the scripture was fulfiled that says, "Abraham believed God, and it was credited to him as righteousness," and he was called God's friend (James 2:23-24).

On one occasion, the Ammonites and Moabites, descendants of Lot by his two daughters, allied with the Meunites to launch an attack on Judah. The king, Jehoshaphat called the people to fast and pray. They came from every town in Judah, gathered before the Lord's temple and Jehoshaphat cried out to God. Listen to him.

> Lord, the God of our ancestors, are you not the God who is in heaven? You rule over all the kingdoms of the nations. Power and might are in your hand, and no one can withstand you. Did you not, our God, drive out the inhabitants of this land before your people Israel, and give it forever to the descendants of Abraham your friend? (2 Ch 20:6).

He pointed out to the Lord that He Himself had given Israel that land. Furthermore, He had forbidden Israel, on their way into the Promised Land, from attacking the

Ammonites and the Moabites. And the Israelites had left them alone. Now the same people were repaying them with evil. But notice he draws God's attention to whom he and his people were, the 'descendants of Abraham your friend'. As for their opponents, they were the descendants of Lot who went away from Jehovah to dwell in Sodom.

The covenant between God and Abraham was an everlasting covenant. Everyone who is in Christ has a share in it. The 'seed' of Abraham through whom the nations will be blessed is none other than Christ Himself. So Abraham stands out as an example and a father. If you are in Christ, you are a child of Abraham. Abraham was a remarkable man of strong faith, extraordinary courage, and resilience. He was imperfect, but he was devoted. We want to know why God called him a friend and what we can emulate in his lifestyle that will give the Father pleasure.

We are indebted also to Moses, a man to whom God spoke face to face as a man speaks to a friend. From him, we learn about holy desire for God. These men dwelt in the hallowed heights of communion with God.

> Who among our sinful race can be worthy of the friendship of Jehovah? Only His Grace can make it possible for any man to walk with God in high companionship.[2]
> Charles Spurgeon

The apostles enjoyed that grace. These men and the

---

2   Spurgeon, C. H. (1969). The Metropolitan Tabernacle pulpit: Sermons preached and revised in 1887. London: Banner of Truth Trust

women who followed them and ministered to the Lord's needs walked with the incarnate Christ daily for three years. The apostle John leaned on his breast, showing the closeness between Jesus and His disciples. Jesus also had one friend called Lazarus whom He had raised from the dead. Lazarus' earlier claim to fame was that he was a friend of the Lord as were his two sisters. The man Jesus embodied the intimacy the Father desires with His creation. The 15th chapter of John has many references to this state of friendship between Jesus and His disciples. This chapter offers clear direction on what it takes to be a friend of God. Can I hope to be a friend of God? Absolutely.

Restoration to friendship in Christ

And to those hallowed heights and far beyond we are called to ascend under the New Covenant. When a person turns from their past wickedness, becomes a follower of Jesus and enters the kingdom, they receive the ability to commune with God. They have 'passed from death to life', they are 'forgiven', they are 'justified' and, they are 'reconciled with God' or as the NLT puts it, they are 'restored to friendship'.

> For if, while we were God's enemies, we were reconciled to him through the death of his Son... (Romans 5:10).

We used to be enemies of God. Jesus, through His death on the cross, effected our reconciliation. What happens when you are reconciled to a person to whom you used to be an enemy? You cease to be an enemy; you become a friend. At the very least, the dispute, discord, disagreement that was a hindrance to true friendship is removed and you can now move ahead and build a solid friendship. That is the condition of the born-again person. He is restored to a state of friendship with God. The New Living Translation of the above Scripture says:

> For since our friendship with God was restored by the death of his Son while we were still his enemies, we will certainly be saved through the life of his Son (Romans 5:10 NLT).

Because of Christ Jesus that enmity has now been removed, and the friendship restored. We must be in awe as we seek to live out the fullness of this friendship. There are two extremes among believers that we need to avoid. Some glibly call God their Friend while barely communing with Him; while others deem it sheer blasphemy to reduce the Divine Being to a condition of friendship with a vile, unworthy human such as they. The truth is infinitely lovelier.

The truth is that we were saved to become friends of God. Yet we can live like faithful friends or like fair-weather friends. We can revel in our new relationship with God and the fact that we are precious to God, without ever asking ourselves if God is precious to us. This new positioning in redemption, obtained by the blood of Jesus—what have we done about it? We cannot be satisfied with our judicial status. It must become your daily experience; your heart and conduct must reflect your relationship with God. God must like what He sees in you.

Consider Abraham

True friendship is one of the sweetest things on the face of the earth and is very beneficial for both parties. The question is, 'what was it about Abraham that God liked'? Relationship with God is enjoyable; it is profitable, not an inconvenience imposed on mankind in exchange for escaping hell. It is not a relationship between equals and does not altogether parallel human friendships. The truth of the matter is that divine friendship is offered to us for our good. And every believer should normally live for nothing else. However, we live in a fallen world where the things of God are alien to us.

So we must cry out for a heart that wants the right things, intimacy with God and friendship with God. To spur you on to holy desire, we shall begin by looking at the impact Abraham's friendship with God had on his life. Every good thing God desires from us is a fruit of a good thing He had previously given to us. God showed Abraham great kindness and we shall see how God treated His friend. As we dwell on the different areas in which God's friendship with Abraham shined forth, let it stir you up to greater expectation in your friendship with God. And in part two we shall seek to elucidate the character traits, the conduct, and the attitude towards God that made a mere man be called a friend of God.

BOOK ONE - AN EXTRAORDINARY LIFE

BOLA OLIVIA OGEDENGBE

PREFACE

TEN GENERATIONS FROM THE FLOOD, EVIL HAD once again gained dominance in the minds of men and in the earth. Here and there, righteous men still lived, but most, unfortunately, had regressed into idolatry. Yet God's plan to redeem mankind was still in motion. So, centuries before Calvary, God found the man through whose descendants the Messiah would come. He found a man who would be true to His covenant. He tested his loyalty, and he was not found wanting. And God blessed him.

As we think about Abraham's friendship with God, we cannot but be moved by the substantial benefits it brought to Abraham's existence. The Most High God revealed Himself to Abraham, he chose to follow and his story was forever changed. Challenges, difficulties, victories, joy awaited him and in all of it, he remained true to God and God to him. Despite the complexities of his existence, his life was marked at every turn by divine favour and blessing. God took good care of His friend. The prophet Isaiah speaking for God left this testimony:

> Listen to me, you who pursue righteousness and who seek the Lord: Look to the rock from which you were cut and to the quarry from which you were hewn; look to Abraham, your father, and to Sarah, who gave you birth. When I called him he was only one man, and I blessed him and made him many (Isaiah 51:1-2).

'I blessed him' said the Lord. Abraham's life, as we shall see, attested to the blessings of divine friendship. All the children of Abraham have access to the same blessings. If we adopt the attitude of Abraham in his dealings with God, what is to stop us from living this same life of abundant outpouring of divine grace?

1

ACCESS TO DIVINE SECRETS

For if while we were God's enemies, we were reconciled to him through the death of his Son, how much more, having been reconciled, shall we be saved through his life! (Romans 5:10).

FRIENDS HAVE ACCESS TO DIVINE SECRETS

'HAD I KNOWN' IS AN OFTEN-HEARD EXPRESSION of regret. So many things would be different in our lives if we had known beforehand what would happen. We would have gone to university, preached to a friend, moved to China, changed professions, and married someone else. The one Person who does know and well in advance is God. Abraham benefited from God's foreknowledge.

Looking to Abraham

A man of seventy-five moves house and home to start a new life in a new location. Generations later his descendants end up possessing the place and his seed becomes a blessing to the entire world. A product of human logic? Assuredly not. Someone knew in advance; someone planned for it to happen. And that someone told His friend, positioned him and worked with him to cause it to happen. But God reveals divine secrets to those He has picked as His friends, and who say yes, as Abraham did.

We see it when the fate of Sodom and Gomorrah was being decided because of their sins. The kings of those cities did not give audience to Abraham, nor call him for consultation. They probably would never have given him the time of day. But the One who is superior to them all, with whom Abraham had a relationship decided to share the information with him. Technically, it was no business of his, but God chose to tell him. He said He could not keep this from Abraham because he would be a great nation and all the nations of the earth would be blessed through him.

Contrast this with the situation of his nephew Lot. Lot dwelt inside the city of Sodom, a place targeted for destruction, but he remained oblivious to the fact. Yet the Bible calls him a righteous man, which would imply that he at least also believed in the God of Abraham. It was because God chose to reveal his plans to Abraham that Abraham was able to entreat Him to change those plans.

God informed Abraham of things present and things in the distant future. He revealed the destiny of his descendants to him. He told him that they would be in Egypt for 400 years. Then in the fourth generation, they would return to the land promised to Abraham.

Prior to this, God had taken the initiative to reiterate to the still childless Abraham His promise to make him a great nation. On hearing that, Abraham complained that God had not given him a child and his servant would be his heir. God said, not so. Then to confirm His word, He made a covenant with Abraham. He put him into a deep sleep and that is when He revealed to him what would happen to his descendants.

> As the sun was setting, Abram fell into a deep sleep, and a thick and dreadful darkness came over him. Then the Lord said to him, "Know for certain that for four hundred years, your descendants will be strangers in a country not their own and that they will be enslaved and mistreated there. But I will punish the nation they serve as slaves, and afterward they will come out with great possessions. You, however, will go to your ancestors in peace

and be buried at a good old age. 16 In the fourth generation, your descendants will come back here, for the sin of the Amorites has not yet reached its full measure (Genesis 15:12-16).

Notice the specifics: they will be ill-treated and enslaved, and then they will leave with many goods. That, of course, is exactly what happened. Why is this important? Because without this information, Abraham, knowing he had been promised the land could have made his son swear never to leave it because it was their inheritance. Then Isaac would have done the same with Jacob and Jacob and family would have died in the land when famine struck. They would have rather died than leave as the word of the Lord was that the land was theirs. Abraham, privy to divine secrets gave no such instruction and Jacob was not held back from moving his family to safety and provision in Egypt.

How many ways do we hinder our own lives and make decisions that harm our children's destiny because we fail to see what God is doing and what God is showing us?

I HAVE CALLED YOU FRIENDS

> I have called you friends, for everything that I learned from my father I have made known to you (John 15:15).

Picture the astonishment of Jesus's disciples when He made this statement. The One they called 'Master' was calling them His friend. Indeed they had been privy to divine truth. They stood head and shoulders above their contemporaries in understanding and insight. They walked with Jesus and saw Him as none else in their generation did. They performed miracles while others gawked; sat with Him and heard glorious things of the age to come. They learnt how man was to live and walk with God and saw first-hand the testimony of the goodness of God to mankind because they were with Him.

The Bible says that 'the secret counsel of the Lord is for those who fear Him, and He reveals His covenant to them,' (Psalm 25:14).

As a friend of God, you can have clarity of understanding. Jesus told the disciples what He received from the Father. He promised us that the Holy Spirit will take from Him, Jesus and reveal to us. There are things that mortal man on his own can never perceive, things that 'eye has not seen and ear has not heard,' but which God the Holy Spirit will show to those who walk with God. There is a higher dimension of revelation for those who walk intimately with God as friends of God. He reveals things about us, things that will happen, national events and things about God.

God gives us a spirit of wisdom and revelation in the knowledge of God. As we know Him, we hear Him. God prepared Abraham for the future; He will prepare you for things to come. See God telling Abraham about his descendants up to four generations. Yet many parents actively oppose God's will for their children because they do not understand what God wants them to do. God is willing to show His friends the right direction in life for themselves and their children, and give them all relevant and vital information for faith, holiness, truth, and godliness.

Today I know that God communicates with His friends, that when we are sensitive, we can receive understanding from God. It was not always so. When I was a young believer, one of my friends would sometimes tell the others in our group of friends that God spoke to her. She occasioned much merriment as we found it rather strange that anyone would say that God spoke to them. I was raised Anglican and God did not speak to Anglicans, or at least my brand of unregenerate Anglicans. Later, I came to realise that God does communicate with us. He speaks through His Word, but also in visions and dreams. He speaks through impressions, what we call the still, small voice etc (always, of course in line with His Word). I also realised that He had been speaking to me since my conversion but I did not see or describe it as my friend did.

We need to know what God has for us. I look back at my life today and realise that nothing is as I imagined it in my teenage years. And yet it is a product of hearing God say 'move here', 'do this', 'start this', and so on and so forth. I know the very place in London, England where He directed me to go on television. I remember the room where I was in Seville, Spain and the chair I was sitting in when He gave directions about the Internet ministry. I remember the specific period when He spoke with me about the audio ministry. I also remember the precise time ten years later after giving up my career when He compelled me to write. I know where I was in South America when He spoke of starting the church ministry. These things were His idea to carry out His purpose and bless those who are willing to take part. Apart from the writing, the rest are light years away from my original idea about my life.

God does not keep His children in ignorance. He reveals Himself and also His plans. A friend of God need not fear what the future holds. You need not fear failure, ageing, accidents, plane crashes, or any potential mishap. God told Abraham he would live to a ripe old age and die happy. He desires no less for you. You have His promise of long life. Believe that you will die happy and that you will have the joy of fulfilling your destiny.

Abraham heard a lot from God but kept it to himself. He did not broadcast it to the neighbours. God went as far as to make a covenant with him to convince him He would indeed give him the land. However, Abraham knew better than to go round telling the current inhabitants that he would expel them from the land. He may not have lived to tell the story. Some people do not hear from God because they talk too much. God speaks to people who can hold their tongue. People try to act important by claiming God told them things that He never said. They sacrifice true revelation for self-exaltation. It is a poor exchange. As a friend of God, God will share His heart with you, but you must know when to speak and when to be silent.

BOLA OLIVIA OGEDENGBE

2

Divine Interaction

I no longer call you servants, because a servant does not know his master's business. Instead, I have called you friends, for everything that I learned from my Father I have made known to you (John 15:15).

FRIENDS ENJOY CONTINUOUS INTERACTION WITH AND REVELATION OF GOD

THE BEAUTY OF A MAN'S LIFE IS in proportion to his interaction with and revelation of God. God likes to show Himself to His own. This great, infinite, unknowable God likes to make Himself accessible. He said that if we seek Him, we will find Him. Many do not believe that. They think no one can know for sure who God is or what God is like, but God guarantees His self-revelation.

Interaction with Abraham

Here is a man living in a community of worshippers of sundry deities in Ur of the Chaldees. There, according to Stephen in Acts 7:2-4 the Most High God appears to Him and calls him. He hears the voice of the Living God and follows Him. He stops at Haran. And God takes him from there to Canaan. God had made him some majestic promises. He had promised to:

- make him a great nation
- bless him
- make his name great
- make him a blessing
- bless those who bless him
- curse those who curse him
- bless all the peoples of the earth through him

He goes from place to place, sets up altars to worship God, and God shows up repeatedly in his life to talk to him, to direct him and to instruct him. The picture is one of consistent and close interaction. And you have to marvel at the extreme benevolence of God towards His friend. That benevolence is a dimension of His character and is unchanging. All His friends enjoy the same benevolence. Unless we understand how intrinsically and infinitely kind and loving God is, we will not wholly receive the encounters He offers us, in His Word and in prayer. His encounters with Abraham are quite instructive.

Abraham obeyed God and left Haran for Canaan. On arrival in Canaan, God appeared to him and told him He would give that land to his descendants. Then after the departure of his nephew Lot, he had yet another encounter with the Lord. The Lord reiterated the promise to give the land to his descendants, who will be too numerous to count. To make sure he understood, God made him look in all four directions and walk the length and breadth of the land.

God reveals Himself to His friends. Picture Abraham. He has conquered the three kings and met with Melchizedek, the priest of the Lord. Now he is minding his business and God gives him a vision. In the vision God reassures Him thus, 'I am your shield, your very great reward' (Genesis 15:1), promising protection and provision. The Holman Christian Standard Bible (HCSB) says 'your reward will be very great'. Abraham interacts with God in the vision. He raises the issue of his childlessness and receives assurance from God. God instructs him to lay two pieces of symbolic covenant elements on the ground.

Then God puts him to sleep and causes a smoking torch to pass between the elements. He thereby confirms

His unbreakable commitment to Abraham, to keep His word to him and help him. One cannot but marvel at the remarkable condescension of God. He speaks in a language his man could understand, using elements that made sense to him to get His point across. He made a covenant with him. At a later stage, Abraham had another encounter, this time after his mistakes and the birth of Ishmael. When Abram was ninety-nine years old, the Lord appeared to him and spoke to Him. God revealed Himself as the Almighty and enjoined him to be faithful and walk in integrity. He promised to:

• multiply him and make him the father of many nations, changing his name from Abram to Abraham,

• make him very fruitful and the father of nations and kings,

• establish His covenant as an everlasting covenant, to be his God and that of his descendants,

• give him the land as his possession forever.

Then the next year, we are told:

> The Lord appeared to Abraham near the great trees of Mamre while he was sitting at the entrance to his tent in the heat of the day... (Genesis 18:1).

On this occasion, Abraham has a lengthy interaction with the Lord and the angels with Him. He again receives confirmation that Sarah would bear a child. Sarah laughs, thinking it impossible. As the Lord prepares to leave, He tells Abraham about the forthcoming destruction of the cities of the plain. This leads to a profound intercession from Abraham on behalf of those cities.

In this encounter, he discusses his childbirth issues,

major regional issues and his domestic concerns about the future of Ishmael. Ponder this: what would have become of Abraham without this continuous interaction with God? Would he have made it? Somehow, I think not. We do not need to see God in person or to see visions, but we do need to interact with Him on a continual basis.

Genesis 22 recounts another powerful encounter. It says that God tested Abraham and asked him to give Him his son Isaac. This was not God coming to encourage and sustain him, to reveal Himself to him, as was the case before. This was God saying 'I want something from you'. Abraham obeyed and when God saw his obedience, He was moved. God was so moved that His voice rang out from heaven to stop Abraham and to give him a ram to sacrifice. Then He spoke again, and this time He made even more powerful promises than before. Abraham's seed shall bless the whole earth, it is the promise of the Messiah.

Is Abraham a special case? Did he enjoy such interaction with God because he was the father of the faith? No, the testimony of Moses shows it was not so. Moses also enjoyed consistent and continuous interaction with God all his life. From the encounter at the burning bush onward, He lived in the presence of God. His assistant Joshua followed in his footsteps. Before Abraham, there were men like Enoch and Noah who stood out in their generation. He walked with God. Others were content to hear about God and look on at a distance. Yet God has always wanted man, even under the Old Covenant, to be close to Him.

At Sinai, Moses spent 40 days in the presence of God

while his people backslid in the camp below. They had said they could not bear the presence of God, so Moses should talk to God and relay His messages to them. Many Christians live like that today. As for Moses, he wanted more of God and asked, and God accepted to show him a greater dimension of Himself. Moses would not budge if God did not go with them. And go He did.

WE WILL COME TO THEM

> Jesus replied, Anyone who loves me will obey my teaching. My Father will love them, and we will come to them and make our home with them (John 14:23).

God is still offering intimacy and continuous interaction. It is part of our birthright as New Testament believers. The transcendent God has come to us, to abide with us. Flaming torches are no longer necessary, nor the voice speaking from heaven. God Himself has come to dwell with us. So, our fellowship and interaction with Him should be even richer and fuller than what Abraham enjoyed. And all are welcome. At Sinai, the presence of God was terrifying. The people drew back fearful, enjoining Moses to speak to God and relate to them whatever He said. They had no desire for a direct encounter.

The privilege of encounter is available for all in Christ Jesus. Yet many still say 'go and talk to God on my behalf and come back and talk to me.' They will not draw near. We too, like Moses, can keep asking for deeper interaction with Him. That is the privilege of friends. As with Abraham, the presence of God will be with you. The conversation and the counsel of God will be present as you draw nearer and nearer to God.

So how do I deepen my interaction with God?

Jesus has given the Holy Spirit to the New Testament believer to facilitate interaction with God. The Holy Spirit is God who has come to settle with us, so the onus is on us to respond to Him continually. God's plan for the believer is for them to be constantly listening to Him, talking to Him and doing what He wants. When Moses boldly showed God he was interested in a deeper revelation of God, he got what he asked for. If you will show the Lord you want to draw closer to Him and interact more deeply with Him, He will help you.

So we begin by asking. Many people do not ask for God's help. They just protest that they are wired differently, that they are of a more practical bent, as though interaction with God was an impractical thing. Pay attention to the way in which God is directing your life and choose to follow what He shows you. The interesting thing is that these steps to greater interaction are also specific characteristics of people who live as friends of God, and that is the subject of Book Two.

BOLA OLIVIA OGEDENGBE

3

FAVOUR AND INFLUENCE WITH GOD

So when God destroyed the cities of the plain, he remembered Abraham, and he brought Lot out of the catastrophe that overthrew the cities where Lot had lived (Gen. 19.29).

WHEN WE WERE CHILDREN, ONE OF MY siblings would always try to get me to ask our father for things. He would come up innocently to ask if

I wanted something or wanted to do something. If ever I happened to say yes, he would jump on it and press me to go and ask Daddy for us both. We were both children, but he thought I had more favour and influence; I certainly had more 'mouth'. I could present my case most eloquently.

Friends of God do not just have access to God, they have influence with God. Because God is infinite and perfect, He will never act against His own will. Yet for His grace to be released in some situations, someone must ask. He requires those who are His friends to weigh in on the matter and intercede so that He can work all things out according to the counsel of His will. That is another blessing Abraham enjoyed.

ABRAHAM HAD FAVOUR AND INFLUENCE

God appeared to 99-year-old Abraham and reiterated the promise to bless him and prosper his descendants. He had in the meantime acquired Ishmael on his own and must have thought God was referring to his descendants through Ishmael. So he went along with it until God mentioned Sarah having a child. At this point Abraham thought 90 and 100 years old respectively was perhaps a bit too old to have children. So he pleaded for God to bless Ishmael. God pointed out that Ishmael was not the chosen one but He would bless him on Abraham's request.

> And as for Ishmael, I have heard you. Behold, I have blessed him, and will make him fruitful, and will multiply him exceedingly. He shall beget twelve princes, and I will make him a great nation. But

My covenant I will establish with Isaac, whom Sarah shall bear to you at this set time next year (Genesis 17:20-21).

I love the way God said 'I have heard you'. Beloved, you need to know that as you walk with God, He hears you. And those dear to you will receive help because you have favour with God. Even people you do not know will receive help if you bring their case before God.

During his next encounter with God, Abraham had the opportunity to weigh in on a divine decision, after the conversation about Sarah's future experience of motherhood. God chose to inform Abraham of the likelihood that he would judge the cities of the plain for their wickedness. Abraham in response exerted some measure of influence on their behalf calling for mercy. The exchange is captivating. In all humility, like one bargaining in a Nigerian market, he asks for clemency and a stay of judgement if some righteous people were found in the city. He went from 50 to 45, to 40, to 35, to 30, to 20, to 10. To all, God responded yes. Someone said to me once that God did not answer Abraham's prayer and his intercession failed. Not so.

God said yes at every point to Abraham's request and to the conditions he proposed. The problem is that the conditions were not met. Only four people were saved from Sodom; even then, the status of Lot's wife is up for debate. What was she hankering after in Sodom? Why did she look back? The ten righteous were not found. Contrast Lot and Abraham. One was in the city God was going to destroy but was oblivious to it. God neither spoke to Him nor even invited him to intercede for the city. The other was far away and God chose to talk to him

Abraham's favour with God is the reason He spared Lot. After Abraham's intercession failed to save Sodom and Gomorrah, the angels went on to effect judgement on the cities. Lot initially lived outside Sodom, but at some point, he made the poor choice of moving into the city. The Bible calls Lot a righteous man and says that his soul was grieved because of the iniquity in Sodom. However, he stayed on, and he would have perished with them.

> So when God destroyed the cities of the plain, he remembered Abraham, and he brought Lot out of the catastrophe that overthrew the cities where Lot had lived (Gen. 19.29).

God's kindness to His friend led not only to the rescue of Lot and his family but also to the preservation of an entire city. When the angel led Lot and his family out of Sodom, he told him to go to the mountain. Lot in fear asks to flee to a city nearby thinking that by the time he reached the mountain the destruction might catch up with him on the way. The request is granted; he is allowed to flee to the city and the Word of God says that that city was spared because of Lot. That is huge.

God's special possession

Some people function in the natural and do not expect God to act on their behalf. If everyone is catching an epidemic, they believe they are entitled to their share of it. Why would God spare them when He had other things to do? And why would He spare someone else because they ask? It makes no sense. They go through life missing out on the benefits of walking intimately with the heavenly Father. You might think, "Yes, but, Abraham was going to be a great nation. I am just me, nothing special." The Bible disagrees. If you are a believer, this is what it says you are.

> But you are a chosen people, a royal priesthood, a holy nation, God's special possession, that you may declare the praises of him who called you out of darkness into his wonderful light (1 Peter 2:9).

You are God's special possession. God was willing to avert destruction He had intended to execute. How much more will He save people from the destruction of the enemy when His own friends cry out to Him? According to the apostle Paul, Epaphroditus was extremely ill, but the Lord delivered him partly to spare him, Paul sorrow. Lives will be spared because you, a friend of God cries out to God for them. People marked for destruction by the enemy will be saved because you, a child of God, a friend of God asks Him to intervene. We must live with the consciousness of divine favour resting on our lives. 'Do not fear what they fear'. Intercede for your friends and family, despite their unbelief and even wickedness. Intercede for the lost and trust that God will hear you and heed.

Furthermore, everyone must take their proper place before the Lord. Where will you stand—among those facing destruction, among those barely rescued, or among those exercising influence to get people rescued? The defining factor is your relationship with God. Position yourself rightly with God and when evil is befalling everyone around, do not expect to be in the mix. Too often believers who have a covenant with God invite on themselves the same disasters as those who do not know God by imagining that they share the same fate. When the economy is going down, and jobs are being lost, expect that you will be spared because there is no recession in the covenant of which you are a partaker. Choose to expect God's deliverance. It is not because everything is falling apart that your house must fall apart. God makes a distinction between those who are His and those who are not when they believe Him.

Lot had the mentality of many believers today. Despite his deliverance from Sodom, he feared to go to the mountain. Then he was allowed to go to the city, the city was saved because of him; yet he was fearful in the city and fled to live in a cave. He did not trust God to save him from the destruction and he did not trust God to protect him in the city. He did not consider going back to his uncle. At this point, he must have lost everything; no mention is made of his many servants and flocks. He ended up being tricked into incestuous sexual encounters, bringing a curse on his descendants.

I want to be a friend of God. Some people stay far from God to stay close to their friends. It is a poor choice. When God is a distant deity and the consciousness of God is vague, pressure from friends, family, and foes who resent our 'religious' activities can become very intense. We end up giving in to their demands to dial down on the God thing. Yet so many erstwhile inseparable friends and brothers have later on become irreconcilable foes. Friendship with God is the only certainty in a changing world.

4

THE FAITHFULNESS OF GOD - DIVINE INTERVENTION

GOD BY HIS VERY NATURE IS ALWAYS faithful to all. However, those who live close to God experience a greater degree of His faithfulness. Every believer has received peace with God but some walk more in that peace than others. And when one is a friend of God, walking in agreement with God, God has free rein to express His goodness in our lives. Abraham's life was far from perfect. He made a huge blunder in the matter of Ishmael. Perhaps he thought he was cooperating with God for the fulfilment of His promise. He strived all his life to do what God wanted, and he reaped huge dividends from the relationship. God stepped in time and time again to help him.

ONE LONE MAN

There are places today where churches and Internet services are plentiful. At the click of a mouse, the nth preacher is offering blessings, encouragement, deliverance and vociferous prayers. It can be hard to fathom what life was like for one lone man who had heard the voice of God and left everything to follow Him. Yet he still had to survive daily challenges, hostility, and uncertainty while God's promise seemed to tarry. But God was ever-present.

I love the way that God would from time to time show up in Abraham's world and repeat his promise. Then Abraham would get himself into a wretched scrape as he wandered around this land that God told him would one day belong to him and his descendants. And God would bail him out. There was a famine in the land. That clause was not in the contract he had signed with God, but there it was, and he had to do something. So he decided to live by his wits, flee to Egypt and pretend his wife was not his wife to avoid trouble with the locals. Pharaoh, who had an eye for beautiful women, took her into his harem, and that was that. No, not quite.

There are times, even in our own lives when it appears God has not delivered the goods and followed through on His plans. We think we must find a clever way of getting out of the trouble we landed in while ostensibly trying to obey God. And just then, God steps in. That is what happened to Abraham. God visited his anger on Pharaoh and his family. He moved to extricate Sarai and Abraham from their self-inflicted predicament. Despite their errors, they experienced the faithfulness of God.

Imagine his distress as he wandered from place to

place facing possible dangers. In Gerar, he again pretended Sarah was not his wife, only his sister, and she ended up in the palace of Abimelech the king. God stepped in once again and warned Abimelech in a dream. Essentially, He told him "Return the man's wife or you and yours will die." Abimelech had acted in ignorance but he promptly obeyed. He rightly grilled Abraham as to why he had not been forthcoming with him. Abraham's response gives us a glimpse into what this nomadic life following God must have cost him.

Imagine his distress as he wandered from place to place facing possible dangers.

> Abraham replied, 'I said to myself, "There is surely no fear of God in this place, and they will kill me because of my wife." Besides, she really is my sister, the daughter of my father though not of my mother; and she became my wife. And when God caused me to wander from my father's household, I said to her, "This is how you can show your love to me: everywhere we go, say of me, 'He is my brother' (Genesis 19:11-13).

God's friends never lose out. He always finds ways to communicate with them, to support them and prove His faithfulness. Witness God's faithfulness when Abraham and his nephew Lot parted ways. Their huge flocks were causing tension between their herdsmen. Abraham suggested to Lot that they might have to separate to avoid conflict and gave him the choice of the land. Lot jumped at the offer and selected the choice terrains for himself. The call was on Abraham, the land was promised to him, but he had taken Lot with him. The man with the promise watched his family member claim the richest parts of the land and did nothing to stop him. And it was the moment God chose to affirm His unstinting support for Abraham.

Separation can be disheartening. I asked a father once how his son was doing. He replied that his son was an adult now and was doing his own thing. You could see that though he thought it right that the young man should have his own life, there was still a twinge of disappointment at the perceived neglect of himself. Sometimes it is natural children who grow up and become excessively independent, distant and uncaring. Sometimes it is children in the Lord who become Absalom, who walk away and assassinate the character of their spiritual parents. A pastor can look at his congregation and wonder where all the people he spent years investing his life in have gone.

The devil will choose that moment to show up to remind him it is no use; human beings are mean, wicked and ungrateful. He will tell him 'throw in the towel, go and do your own thing; you could be successful in the world, so why bother with ministry?' A businessman can close the door to his office after struggling to keep his business afloat for months and hear that same voice saying, 'there is no point; just give up'. But at those moments, a friend of God will hear another voice. He will hear God saying 'I am with you, it is not the end; it is but the beginning. I will fulfil the promise'.

Alone in a foreign land, still childless, with the only

family member now gone, Abraham would not have been jumping for joy. He was prosperous, but he had no offspring of his own. Lot was the son of another and he was gone. But his friend, the Lord Himself chose that moment to show up. And what an encounter! Note this: the Bible says that Lot looked around and saw the part of the land that was well watered, that looked like the garden of the Lord, and he chose it. But when God showed up, He told Abraham to 'look around' to the left, right, south, north, east, west; and that He would give him all the land that he saw. He made him look out over the whole land including the part the nephew had claimed and promised it would all be his.

Yet when Lot was taken captive after the city of his abode was sacked by a foreign army, the uncle he left behind was the one who rushed to his rescue. After this event, God showed Himself faithful once again. He visited Abraham, reiterated His promises and made a solemn covenant with him. He thus pledged to be faithful to Abraham and his descendants for generations to come. Someone might say, 'well, I am no Abraham.' True, the destiny of humanity hinged on this one man following God faithfully. Yet God's dealings with him are not an isolated case, far from it. They are an illustration of His faithfulness toward anyone who responds in like manner to His call.

The kindness and faithfulness of God extended to the descendants of His friend. Even the son born out of the plan of God received special attention from God. The plan had not changed. Ishmael would not be the son of the promise through whom God's plan would come.

However, because he was still Abraham's son, he would be blessed. Imagine living a life whereby people close to you receive special grace from God, for your sake. That is the portion of every New Testament believer who is, according to God's Word a son and daughter of Abraham. That is the portion of those whom Jesus calls His friends, you and I.

God will sustain His friends through difficulties, and He will cause them to overcome. Abraham solved his own problem of childlessness while Sarah remained childless. And God showed up to fulfil His original plan. First, He spoke to Abraham and reiterated His promises.

> As for me, this is my covenant with you: you will be the father of many nations. No longer will you be called Abram; your name will be Abraham, for I have made you a father of many nations. I will make you very fruitful; I will make nations of you, and kings will come from you. I will establish my covenant as an everlasting covenant between me and you and your descendants after you for the generations to come, to be your God and the God of your descendants after you. The whole land of Canaan, where you now reside as a foreigner, I will give as an everlasting possession to you and your descendants after you; and I will be their God (Genesis 17:4-8).

You know how we sometimes interpret God's words our way because they seem so implausible. So Abraham asked God to bless Ishmael. When he heard God mention Sarah, he laughed, thinking Sarah was too old. How could she have a child? But God was insistent that Sarah would have the child. That was the plan and God had the power to bring it to pass. When God repeats a promise, He has every intention of fulfilling it. He is not rewinding the tape. Sarah would have the child, and she did. Whatever impossibilities you are looking at now, remember that whatever God has said about it is bound to happen.

Well, the next year God encountered Abraham and stayed for a good while to talk to him. He reiterated the promise about Sarah. To avoid any doubt as to how astonishing this miracle would be, the passage tells us that Abraham and Sarah were old. Not only that, but Sarah could no longer nurse any hopes of having children as she was past childbearing age. So when she heard the Lord speak, well, she thought it extremely odd, and she laughed to herself. Genesis 18, verse 12 tells us:

> So Sarah laughed to herself as she thought, 'After I am worn out and my lord is old, will I now have this pleasure?'

God's comment is highly instructive and worth its weight in gold.

> Then the Lord said to Abraham, 'Why did Sarah laugh and say, "Will I really have a child, now that I am old?" Is anything too hard for the Lord? I will return to you at the appointed time next year, and Sarah will have a son (Genesis 18:13-14).

You have to marvel at God, because He said, 'Why did Sarah laugh?' You and I will say, 'Why would Sarah not laugh?' But for God, it is simple. He is God and nothing is too difficult for Him to do. He is not limited by age,

He made the human body, He can restore and rejuvenate it if need be. He is subject to no law and limited by no circumstance.

I believe that a person walking in divine friendship needs to buy himself a very good pillow and sleep like a baby. Every promise of God for your life is bound to come to pass. After all, is anything too hard for God? That is a blanket statement of divine possibilities that every believer must appropriate. Speak it to yourself continually, make it a song, dance to it, whatever, just hold on to it. And when everything threatens to fall apart, remember whose you are.

God's blessings extend to every area of life for His friends. We have seen how God blessed Lot, the nephew, as well as Ishmael, the child of Abraham's flesh; and when Isaac came forth, he too was blessed because of his father. He was born, the Bible tells us (Gen 21.2) at the time set by God which He told Abraham about. We see that some issues in our lives may be delayed, but some are a matter of divine timing. Even the boy's marriage was divinely orchestrated. There is a grace over a child of God working in friendship with God that even those close to them recognise.

When Abraham sent his servant to find his son a wife, the undertaking was uncertain, to say the least, but the servant who had lived with Abraham for so many years knew that his master had a God who was faithful. I pray that you will experience the faithfulness of God to such a degree in your life that your co-workers, family members, friends, employees will know that your God is with you. Abraham's servant said this prayer:

> Then he prayed, 'Lord, God of my master Abraham, make me successful today, and show kindness to my master Abraham. See, I am standing beside this spring, and the daughters of the townspeople are coming out to draw water. May it be that when I say to a young woman, "Please let down your jar that I may have a drink," and she says, "Drink, and I'll water your camels too" – let her be the one you have chosen for your servant Isaac. By this, I will know that you have shown kindness to my master (Genesis 24:12-14).

WHAT WAS THE OUTCOME?

His prayers were answered. Before he could conclude his prayer, a young woman came out, whose name was Rebekah, and she did everything he had requested of God. This was no coincidence as she was also the daughter of Bethuel, a relative of Abraham's. What a wonderfully faithful God.

What comes to mind when you think of Abraham? Childlessness, wandering, faith, sacrifice, etc. What else? Blessing, wealth, divine assistance; and rightly so. Through the challenges of his life, God was present. He was blessed and tested by God in the matter of Isaac and he passed the test. His servant said, in introducing himself to Rebekah's family:

> So he said, 'I am Abraham's servant. The Lord has blessed my master abundantly, and he has become wealthy. He has given him sheep and cattle, silver and gold, male and female servants, and camels and donkeys...' (Genesis 24:34-35).

There is something remarkable when the people around us can testify of God's goodness to us and blessing on our lives. Many would say that God provided for people materially under the Old Covenant but under the New, he leaves us to struggle without stepping in to help; that is illogical. God consistently provided for Abraham. Similarly, every child of God can expect divine provision for His life. Many seek God for money, for fame, for peace and other sundry self-centred needs'. However, when our desires are for God, He will give Himself to us and provide peace, rest, and other such needs. Jesus made it so clear; one wonders why we miss it.

Jesus said our focus and desire must be for the things of God, and all other things, needs et al. will be added to us. That is a promise that if we will love God for Himself and focus on divine priorities, our needs will be taken care of. Where is your focus? It is our choice to be friends of God. We must cry out to God to change our selfish hearts and fill us with desire for God and to be friends with God.

Abraham's childbearing issues would recede into the distant past. The man who for 85 years had been childless later married Keturah and had other children. Amazing God! God's solutions will outlast any problem. At the end of his life, this is the testimony borne of God's dealings with him.

Abraham lived a hundred and seventy-five years. Then Abraham breathed his last and died at a good old age, an old man and full of years; and he was gathered to his people (Genesis 25:7-8).

He died satisfied, having fulfilled his purpose in God's plan. That is God's desire for every one of His children.

BOLA OLIVIA OGEDENGBE

Epilogue

NONE OF US ARE CALLED TO SPEND our existence admiring the lives of others. We are to learn from them, be inspired by them and move on to accomplish great things with our own lives. Intimacy with God will ensure that we are fully conscious of God's purpose for us. We will please the Father as we live in accordance with His heart. We will enjoy His help and provision in the challenging times of life and we will be armed with the understanding required to live such as to honour Him. This understanding comes from His Word and the Spirit of God pours it into our hearts.

I also find personally that friendship with God is a major protection from sin. There are places where I would have gone, things I would have done that I chose to forgo because I loved God. I did not want to displease Him and did not want to sour the beautiful relationship that we had.

I encourage you today to step into this call to friendship, embrace it wholeheartedly. Nothing that you have to give up to get close to God is worth having. If it conflicts with intimacy, it has no place in your life. Take the necessary steps and you will never have a moment of regret.

If you need help along the way, in understanding and taking these steps, go on to the next part of this work. In Book Two, 'Becoming a friend of God', we will examine at length Abraham's character, conduct and attitude. What was his secret? What was it about this man that God would call him His friend? What are the characteristics of a man or woman who would be a friend of God? We will also bring on board other people like Moses, Enoch, etc. And finally, we shall also dwell extensively on the Lord Jesus Himself and His intimacy with the Father.

BOOK TWO - BECOMING A FRIEND OF GOD

PREFACE

WE HAVE NO MORE PRESSING NEED THAN to attune our hearts to God and become men and women He can boast about. When many people think of Abraham, they think 'father of a nation', they think 'father of the faithful', they think 'man of great wealth', and rightly so. But I insist that the greatest quality and blessing of Abraham was that God considered him a friend. And that is the greatest thing God can say about you and I.

Bear in mind that when God gives you anything, it is not because you deserve it but because He is good. But when God calls you His friend, it is not only because He is good, but because He has seen some things in you that please Him. Of course, we can only become what He makes us, but unless we become, we cannot be His friends.

So what did Abraham become? What are the specific characteristics of this man? What did God work through in his life such that God could call him His friend? That is what we are about to examine. The new birth gives us access to divine friendship. How close that friendship becomes depends on what we do and become. Jesus called His disciples His friends, for specific reasons. What are those? Let's embark on a fresh journey into the heart of God's will for us.

2.1

Know Him

But more than that, I count everything as loss compared to the priceless privilege and supreme advantage of knowing Christ Jesus my Lord [and of growing more deeply and thoroughly acquainted with Him—a joy unequaled]. For His sake I have lost everything, and I consider it all garbage, so that I may gain Christ (Phil. 3:8 (AMP)).

TRUE FRIENDSHIP IS PREDICATED UPON A DEGREE of knowledge. Some people have thought themselves as friends until they got to know each other, whereupon they considered that foregoing that particular acquaintance was no loss to them. The enchantment melted away as they saw the other in their true colours. With God the opposite is true. Some knowledge of God is required for true friendship; the better we know Him the more attached to Him we become and the more we manifest the other attributes of true friendship.

To begin with, God opened the door to deep knowledge to us in the new birth. We came in the door and some promptly took their seat there while others ventured in further to discover the fullness of the relationship. It is a blessing to desire God. Of course, we all come to God for basically selfish reasons, or perhaps I should say most, decide for yourself which you think theologically accurate. Some issue, dissatisfaction, questioning, trial, etc. pushed us to begin asking the right questions, and we finally ended up in the arms of God. Or perhaps we were confronted with our own sinfulness and the not too enticing prospect of eternal separation from God and we scuttled for shelter in the kingdom. But know Him we must if we will be His friends.

Here is how we break this down. Friends of God know His identity. Friends of God know His nature. Friends of God know His desires, purposes, and expectation. That is where we begin. We begin with the knowledge of God.

KNOW HIS IDENTITY

In knowing Him, the first dimension is to know His identity. In our generation, there is a blurring of the lines. We live, many of us, in secular societies that have spiritual overtones. We also live in pluralistic societies with multiple religions occupying the same sacred space. For fear of displeasing anyone, we sometimes seek to define a generic divine being we can all relate to that is not the exclusive preserve of a particular group or locked into some specific form of revelation. For others, God is an impersonal force.

So when you hear 'God' it can mean many things. However you cannot have a relationship with an impersonal force, nor can you be friends with a person of undefined identity. A God who can be anything is not a God to whom we can relate. Many Christians have bought into that perspective and it has wreaked havoc on their relationship with God or capacity to know Him. We can relate in intimacy with a Person but not an idea, and many are now serving the idea of God rather than the Person of God. This knowledge is crucial. That is why God took pains to continue to affirm His identity and speak of it to show His people who He was. How has He revealed Himself and what is His identity?

Moses had a dramatic life-changing encounter with God at the burning bush. He saw a bush burning that was not consumed. He decided to step closer and find out what was going on. And then God spoke to him audibly. He mandated him to go back to Egypt, from where he had fled in ignominy forty years before, on a rescue mission for His people. Despite the power of that encounter, Moses still had a question. 'Who should I say sent me'? In other words, what is Your identity? And God obliged by giving His identity.

When Saul had his famous Damascus road encounter, he asked a similar question 'Who are you, Lord?' He was a Pharisee, a great religious leader, a man who believed he knew God, but stunned at this encounter, he knew he needed more insight into this divine Personage. Jesus obliged him and said He was Jesus, whom Paul was persecuting. How clear and direct. God likes to reveal Himself.

The question is 'who is your God'? I think it is a question modern evangelicals need to be asking yet again as we are in grave danger of adopting the god of the 'Canaanites' and making a golden calf whom we call 'Elohim'. It is essential that we know His identity not only from a theological and intellectual perspective but also for the purposes of daily living by faith. It was recognition of the identity of Jesus that moved the apostle Paul to forsake all he once held dear, to take the gospel to the entire Roman world and to cry out with such aching desire 'that I might know' Him.

Most in the modern world will perhaps not assimilate the God of our Lord Jesus Christ to gods of wood and clay. However, we are already confusing His identity with that of the mental gods of our age, those hybrid and neutered deities of spirituality that promise all and require nothing. They are fashioned not by the hands of men but by their imagination and pen and paper to be as inoffensive, pleasing and generic as possible. They are Antichrists who negate the need for an exclusive Saviour who forgives sins. A weak church that seeks to flee the ire of its generation will increasingly succumb to this temptation at the expense of its spiritual vitality. But you are to be a friend of God and not an imaginer of divine possibilities. So be clear as to His identity.

Abraham knew Him. I often wondered how well a primitive man of idol worshipping stock could know the Lord God Elohim. And unlike David we do not have lofty descriptions of Jehovah from the pen of Abraham, nor do we have moving expressions of adoration from him. But know God he did. He distinguished between this God and the multiplicity of deities worshipped in his home area of Ur, in Mesopotamia. He did not succumb to the temptation to marry Him with the gods of the Canaanites and Amorites, or the gods of Egypt and Zoar. God revealed Himself to Abraham. Who leaves home and family to head for an unknown place following an unknown deity?

The destination was unknown but the God taking him was not. The same applies to us if I am permitted to digress. What we are most in need of is not the finest detail about every divine direction as we voyage through life, rather it is an intimate knowledge of the One steering the ship of our existence. We may not always know where we are headed, but we must know Who is sending us and going with us because He holds the compass and the map.

The purpose of God is often hindered by the fact that believers are not willing to step out into the unknown. They are not willing to trust God to work things out in their lives and in the church. When we know the One who is behind us and the One who is carrying us, we will be willing to do anything that He says irrespective of the apparent attendant risks or difficulties. Too often once we face a challenge, we begin to moan, grumble, doubt and fuss. Are we certain God is in this? What is He doing? Has He lost His eyesight and can He not see what we are dealing with? Is He even there? Is any of this real?

We have the Scriptures as a testimony of the faithfulness of God; we also have a testimony of history showing God's dealings with mankind. We know He can be trusted. Abraham was less privileged than we are. Yet he trusted God. He knew Him and obeyed. Is it any wonder that God called him His friend!

Stephen testifies in Acts 7.12 concerning Abraham. He affirms that God called him to leave his family and his country when he was in Ur of the Chaldees and took him to live in the country where they now lived.

> To this he replied: 'Brothers and fathers listen to me! The God of glory appeared to our father Abraham while he was still in Mesopotamia before he lived in Harran. "Leave your country and your people," God said, "and go to the land I will show you." So he left the land of the Chaldeans and settled in Harran. After the death of his father, God sent him to this land where you are now living (Acts 7:2-4).

Do you see that? When God called him, he was alone with his little family and childless to boot. Isaiah 51 expresses it well. He was called alone and God blessed and multiplied him. Consequently, by the time Stephen was speaking, the descendants of Abraham now inhabited the land. He knew God. In Genesis 14.22 Abraham describes his God. The king of Sodom had just offered him spoil following on Abraham's defeat of the enemies of this king. Abraham declines the offer saying:

> With raised hand I have sworn an oath to the Lord, God Most High, Creator of heaven and earth, that I will accept nothing belonging to you, not even a thread or the strap of a sandal, so that you will never be able to say, "I made Abram rich" (Genesis 14:22-23).

Why? He knew his God; the name on His business card was clear 'Master of the heavens and the earth'. He knew Him so well that he turned down riches so that his God would not be dishonoured. When we know God, we cannot be bought, intimidated or put down.

God likes to reveal His identity. We cannot take this lightly as it is only by revelation that the understanding of His identity and singularity will take root in our hearts. Indeed, nothing in our experience is even remotely akin to the identity and personality of God. Consequently, to know Him, we must decide that we want to know Him and seek Him out. Like Paul, we must determine that 'my goal is to know Him'.

KNOW HIS CHARACTER

Not only do we need to be clear as to His identity, but we also need to know His character. For many people, knowing God means they are saved, and they have tender thoughts towards their sweet heavenly Father even though their picture of Him is somewhat fuzzy. It is akin to someone gazing wistfully at a faded photograph of old friends. Knowing His character is not about sentiments, but about the deep-seated understanding of His nature and Person.

So we know His identity and we also need to know His nature. The attributes of God declare the character of God. It is worth taking time to meditate on them. What is God like? I cannot be His friend if I do not know what He is like. Have you ever felt that deep in your heart you were slightly suspicious of God's intentions? Don't you sometimes feel that we 'tolerate' God? We suspect He will change our good plans for our lives and impose things on us that may not be quite so palatable. We almost love Him 'despite His unorthodox ways'. I do not expect you to admit it (most of us will not), but we are too often wary about following anything we sense He is saying to us unless, of course, He spells out in black and white exactly how it will all turn out. Why? Because we do not know His character.

I. Knowledge of the character of God is essential to being a friend of God.

It is essential for us to be as God wants and to do what God wants. We will never become intimate with the Lord if we do not know and like His character. In our Foundations class for new believers, there is a class on God that deals extensively with the attributes of God. It is an opportunity for new believers and new arrivals in the church to meditate extensively on the nature and character of God as revealed in the Scriptures.

They can flesh out the picture of God as presented

in the Scriptures and be delivered from mental barriers and erroneous perceptions of the identity and character of God, the God of our Lord Jesus Christ. This is more than a purely theological or academic exercise. What we believe about God determines how close we ever will be to him whether we draw near enough to become true friends and what as friends we are willing to do for Him.

II. Knowledge of the character of God triggered Abraham's obedience.

Question. Why did Abraham accept to give up his son, Isaac after having previously let go of Ishmael at God's request? Simple. Because he knew God, and he knew God's character. The Bible tells us that he believed that God was able to bring Isaac back from the dead. He judged that God was good, that God was faithful, and that God would not leave him childless. And he was right. Because he knew Him, he listened to Him, trusted Him, and obeyed Him. On such weighty life issues, he stumbled, yet eventually passed with flying colours.

Compare that to how modern believers agonise for days, weeks, even months over simple instructions they receive in prayer or see in Scripture. Am I sure that God directed me to join the early morning prayer meeting? I sense He wakes me up at night to pray, so should I do it? Or maybe it is the devil trying to make me pray more so I will start trusting in my works rather than leaning on grace? Besides, how will I function at work the next day? Then different Bible interpretations are brought into play to highlight nuances in translation to let us off the hook. We do the Scriptures a worse disservice than liberal scholars and unbelieving critics.

No doubt Abraham was less than delighted at the prospect of letting go of his only remaining son, and God took pains to tell him 'your only son'; however his thinking about God was very accurate, and it enabled him to pass the test. The test? Yes, the Bible says that God tested him. Ask yourself these simple questions:

- What are my thoughts about God?
- Are they accurate?
- Does what I think of God encourage me to do what He says and to trust Him?

A. W. Tozer said, "What comes into our minds when we think about God is the most important thing about us.[3]"

The thoughts, the imaginations, the ideas you have about God are the most important thing about your life because they condition your entire life. Abraham thought that God was powerful, good, and trustworthy and it affected his choices.

> Abraham reasoned that God could even raise the dead, and so in a manner of speaking he did receive Isaac back from death (Hebrews 11:19).

The challenge with many in our generation is that we hardly sit down to think about God, and when we do, our thoughts about Him often are superficial. Yet there is immense benefit in taking the time to sit still and think

---

3   Tozer, A. W. The Knowledge of the Holy. James Clarke & Co., , 1965

deeply about God on the basis of what His Word says about Him.

III. Knowledge of the character of God triggers and sustains our praise.

When a person does not know God, their praises are short-lived and their testimonies transitory. His love will make them sing for a season, but with the onset of the slightest turbulence, the song fades away and sorrow and sighing take its place, along with questions about the goodness of God. Can friendship thrive in such an atmosphere? No.

IV. Knowledge of the character of God loosens our purse strings.

A subpar knowledge of God makes tithing and giving to God an enterprise fraught with anxiety and risk. How does one entrust one's money and financial affairs to a little-known deity who might leave one to starve without lifting His divine finger in assistance? When Abraham met God's high priest Melchizedek, one of his acts of worship to God was to present the high priest with a tithe of all the spoil.

He then turned around and refused to take money from the pagan prince of Sodom so God's name would not be defiled. He gave and did not jump on the next opportunity to get something for himself. God's honour was more important, a mark of true friendship. He knew God as a generous giver and knew He would take care of his needs. Quibbling about tithing, backpedalling on tithing or giving because of inadequate 'returns' occurs because of a deficiency in the knowledge of God's character.

V. Knowledge of the character of God promotes intimacy.

Moses also was a man who knew God. He knew God's ways, and the people knew God's acts.

> He made known his ways to Moses, his deeds to the people of Israel: the Lord is compassionate and gracious, slow to anger, abounding in love. He will not always accuse, nor will he harbour his anger forever (Psalm 103:7-9).

Some Christians live in symbiosis, in intimacy with God. Others merely see what He is doing; they see the miracles but do not relate to Him personally. They know neither His heart nor His ways. They merely know His acts. Yet we are called to relate to Him personally, to be caught up in desire for Him. We love the miracles He does and they are good. However, it is in knowing His nature and His desires that we can honour Him and serve Him, and remain faithful to the relationship in times of difficulty.

VI. Knowledge of the character of God will cause us to honour Him in the storms of life.

Paul knew God as truthful. When in the boat on the verge of a shipwreck, while experienced sailors were seeking to flee, he was at peace. He knew his God and his God had sent an angel to him to assure him of safety. He said 'the God whose I am sent His angel' (Acts 27:23). And since He never lies, he, Paul had no reason to fear, despite the virulence of the storm. He remained close to God. And God brought him through.

VII. Knowledge of the character of God births faithfulness in us and causes us to experience His faithfulness.

Daniel knew God was good. He and his people had been taken off to captivity, but he knew God. He chose to adhere to God's laws even though it could jeopardise his promotion in the foreign land to which God had chosen to have his people exiled. Unfavourable circumstances did not cause him to cast aspersions on God's character as we are wont to do, because he knew God's character. He knew his people were bearing the brunt of God's judgement because of their own wickedness. There was no finger-pointing at the Most High.

> Lord, the great and awesome God, who keeps his covenant of love with those who love him and keep his commandments... (Daniel 9:4).

Consequently, he lived a most extraordinary life. His reverence for God remained intact as did his consideration of God's goodness and greatness. Your closeness to God is conditioned by your knowledge of his nature and your admiration of His Person.

KNOW WHAT GOD WANTS

The third thing is that we know what God wants. We know what we want and we tend to be persistent in asking for what we want, but true friends of God will first enquire as to what God wants. This means that divine desire must be the driving force for all human desire. Since God does not exist to do our will but we His, the beauty of our relationship with Him is contingent on our knowing what that will is and complying with it.

Human existence must be a continual unfolding of divine purposes, not simply divine provision for human needs. Put simply, what God has in mind for mankind is revealed in His Word and must become the object of our desire. In so doing we come into a deep-seated harmony with God that results in a profound friendship. I love the passage where Moses speaks to the people of Israel and says,

> And now, Israel, what does the Lord your God ask of you but to fear the Lord your God, to walk in obedience to him, to love him, to serve the Lord your God with all your heart and with all your soul, and to observe the Lord's commands and decrees that I am giving you today for your own good? (Deut. 10:12).

Here we see what God wants them to do, fear, obey, serve, love Him completely. So we can know what God wants. He wants all of us. The Holy Spirit testifies continually to divine desire.

There is also what God wants in specific situations for specific people. God has plans and projects that involve His children. Consequently, every child of God must seek to know where they fit into God's purposes in their generation. Their focus must be on what God requires of them; in a general sense as He does every one of His children, but also in a specific sense as relates to their own calling and circumstances. What does God want to do with me? What does God want me to do?

In an encounter with God, Abraham received a revelation of divine desire. From then on, Abraham knew that God wanted to make him a great nation and give him a mighty inheritance. Do you know what God wants for your life? Do you know what He wants to do with your life? How can you cooperate with Him and be in harmony with Him if you do not know?

Growing in the Knowledge of God

God is self-revealing. He has always gone to great lengths to reveal Himself, His purposes and plans to individuals. As we have seen, Abraham knew God through revelation from God Himself. It started when God called him out of his native land and continued throughout his life.

> When Abram was ninety-nine years old, the Lord appeared to him and said, 'I am God Almighty; walk before me faithfully and be blameless (Genesis 17:1).

Moses knew God through God's direct revelation of Himself as he went about his daily business. He saw a sight of wonder and like most of us, curiosity got the better of him and he decided he had to see what was going on. His life was never the same again. Mark that this was not something that happened there every day nor was it fortuitous that Moses happened to be there at the time. God put the display on specially for him. He knew he would be there, went out to meet him and attracted his attention. Then He spoke to him, gave him an assignment and told him His name. And that was the beginning of a magnificent relationship. Moses lived a life of divine encounters. He lived in very close proximity to God and God spoke to him face to face, the Bible tells us.

> The Lord would speak to Moses face to face, as one speaks to a friend. Then Moses would return to the camp, but his young assistant Joshua son of Nun did not leave the tent (Exodus 33:11).

Samuel knew God through God's self-revelation to Him, he learnt what God wanted. The lad was enjoying a good night's sleep when God broke in on his slumber by calling his name aloud. Naturally, the boy thought the call came from next door and sought out the likely speaker, his guardian, Eli the priest. Eli denied calling him. The third time it happened, it finally dawned on him that God was calling the young man. Eli told Samuel to invite the Lord to speak next time He called. Samuel did and speak the Lord did. He told him about the current state of affairs in the land and what was going to happen. He called Samuel to His service. Remember Job,

> My ears had heard of you but now my eyes have seen you (Job 42:5).

We cannot be His friends if we only know Him by hearsay. Gideon was one man who had heard of God's great works but had seen nothing. And he wanted to know where were all the great works they had heard that God did in the past. It reminds me of a Nigerian chorus that breaks out spontaneously when people see the great works of God:

> "I heard about You mighty God, mighty God, I heard about You, mighty God, mighty God, that is why I am here."

What they are saying is this 'I heard You were great, I came to see and I have indeed seen'. Gideon ended up seeing as well. Daniel knew God through God's self-revelation in His Word, and through dreams and visions learned God's ways. Paul knew God through a direct encounter with the risen Christ, dreams and visions and through the Word. And when he exclaimed 'who are you, Lord'? The Lord responded by identifying Himself, 'I am Jesus, whom you are persecuting'. He also found out what God wanted from him. I think it will be safe to conclude that God wants us to know Him, His nature and His purposes.

I admit I did not always know it was possible to know God. There may be something in the human psyche that persists in consigning God to the realm of the unknowable. His identity to be sure, we can recite by rote. After all, the descendants of Abraham would refer to Him as the God of Abraham, Isaac, and Jacob while, in some instances, still wilfully going their own way. So we too can call Him the God of our Lord Jesus Christ, the Almighty, the Great I am, the Rose of Sharon and laud Him brilliantly in worship while still stubbornly following our own thinking.

But true revelation brings a man to his knees as Abraham fell prostrate before God and binds a man's heart to the Most High. Paul received the identity of Jesus and his world was turned upside down. He became a fervent admirer and ardent pursuer of the purpose of Christ and promoter of His kingdom.

How did Moses become a man with whom God communicated in such a manner? Was it because he had a great assignment? Was it because he enjoyed special favour that was not available to others? One thing stands out in the life of this man. It was his preoccupation with God—knowing Him, honouring Him, serving Him. Preoccupation with God is essential to knowing God. I call it a life of divine desire.

Desire and Ask

To know God, we must desire Him. Something in the heart of every born-again child of God desires to know God. We may suppress it or give it expression, it is up to us. If the Spirit of God dwells in us, we cannot be utterly indifferent to God. So desire is first a choice and then an experience. It means we must be willing to take this route. Then we cry out to the God who enables us to will and to do according to His good pleasure, for a deeper desire for Himself. We then begin to express our longing to know Him. What happened to Paul can and will happen to any person who has been born- again as they have been positioned in Christ in relationship with the Father. Desire fuels persistence and makes you insatiable in the quest for knowledge of God. Think of Paul crisscrossing the Roman Empire preaching Christ from such depths of insight and revelation, yet still saying 'that I might know Him'.

As you grow in knowledge, you grow in desire. Think of a man who has had profound encounters with God still yearning for more. Moses unabashedly cried out to know God. He wanted God to show him the things about God that would enable him to know God as he ought to know Him. God had told him 'I know you; you have found favour with me', and Moses, rather than being satisfied with that, used it as a stepping stone to a powerful request. You know me, Lord, now I want to know You! Is it any wonder that God spoke to him face to face!

> Moses said to the Lord, 'You have been telling me, 'Lead these people,' but you have not let me know whom you will send with me. You have said, 'I know you by name and you have found favour with me.' If you are pleased with me, teach me your ways so I may know you and continue to find favour with you. Remember that this nation is your people' (Exodus 33:12-13).

Do not be satisfied to know that God loves you and that He has favoured you. That is where many people stop. Be like Moses. Cry out to God. Say 'Lord, if I have found favour with you, show me Your ways so that I may know You'. I pray that you will be flooded with divine desire—desire to know God and abide in Him.

One other way of asking is to pray in other tongues. If you are baptised in the Holy Spirit and speak in other tongues, take time to pray extensively in tongues. It makes you more spiritually sensitive and alert and more able to receive understanding from God. God even uses it to bless other people in unusual ways. Let me tell you a story about a prayer meeting I attended many years ago. A good friend had started attending a non-charismatic evangelical church and invited me to a fellowship in the home of one of the young people. We had a short time of prayer and at one point I found myself praying in tongues, then I began to sing in tongues very quietly as these were not boisterous charismatics.

At the end, a young man there of North African extraction who had recently become a Christian spoke to me eagerly. He asked me in what language I had prayed. I explained to him what praying in tongues was. Then he said that he did not understand the words I prayed but as I prayed, he became flooded with the understanding that Jesus was the Son of God. It was like a gradual unfolding before him and he was utterly convinced, and might I say, very happy. This was something he had struggled with before, and in prayer, God had supernaturally communicated that truth to him. Amazing, self-revealing God.

SEE HIM IN HIS WORD

God's Word reveals the Person of God; it shows us the nature of God, the ways and the works of God. One man who shows how powerful God's Word is in revealing the ways of God is Stephen. Abraham did not have the Scriptures but Stephen did and he was an avid student. Indeed when he had to stand before the Sanhedrin and defend himself, he was expansive, exhaustive and knowledgeable on the identity of God, the ways of God and the desires of God. He took them through a lengthy exposition of the theological history of Israel, stage by stage up till the coming of Christ and the new dispensation.

With the Holy Spirit illuminating the Word to us, we

can 'see' Him daily, understand His nature and apprehend His desires. That is why the apostle Paul prayed that remarkable prayer for the recipients of the Ephesian letter. He said this:

> I pray that the eyes of your heart may be enlightened in order that you may know the hope to which he has called you, the riches of his glorious inheritance in his holy people, and his incomparably great power for us who believe (Ephesians 2:18-19).

Continual contemplation of God in His Word is essential to knowing Him. Our eyes must see Him, we need only ask and His Word will be the means of self-revelation. As you study, meditate and ask in prayer, understanding will flood your heart, God will become increasingly real to you.

The Bible is a compendium of divine desire. It was in studying the Scriptures, the writings of the prophet Jeremiah that Daniel knew God wanted His people to return from captivity at that specific time. Jeremiah had prophesied 70 years of captivity and Daniel saw that the time had come. The ways of God were made apparent to him and he began to pray. I love his prayer. This portion is particularly striking:

> Now, our God, hear the prayers and petitions of your servant. For your sake, Lord, look with favour on your desolate sanctuary. Give ear, our God, and hear; open your eyes and see the desolation of the city that bears your Name. We do not make requests of you because we are righteous, but because of your great mercy. Lord, listen! Lord, forgive! Lord,

hear and act! For your sake, my God, do not delay, because your city and your people bear your Name (Daniel 9:17-19).

Daniel is well known for his visions but he was a man of the Word. So was Paul, a great scholar, a lover of God, dreamer and visionary. Even in prison, he asked for books and parchments to be brought to him.

Contemplating Jesus

We know God as we meditate on the Person of Christ. The Bible says that God in the past spoke through the prophets, but in these last days, He has spoken through the Son. The Son is described in Hebrews 1:3 as 'the radiance of God's glory and the exact representation of his being.' Jesus is the revelation of God. If you can contemplate Jesus, you can know God. Jesus said so Himself. At one point Philip asked Jesus to show them the Father, Jesus's response 'Anyone who has seen me has seen the Father. How can you say, 'Show us the Father'? (John 14:9). To contemplate Jesus is to contemplate God. The letter to the Colossians testifies similarly that He is the image of the invisible God. So how do we see God? We focus on Jesus.

Contemplate His past works

Psalm 103 has to be one of the most frequently read psalms in our church services. The psalmist begins by calling on his own soul to bless the Lord. Then he enjoins himself to not forget the Lord's goodness to him and proceeds to list some of those blessings. They include healing, deliverance etc. a most instructive list. The principle applies when it comes to growing in the knowledge of God. We must remember His past dealings with us.

Abraham could not read this Scripture to know God's ways. What he did was keep God's dealings with him at the forefront of his mind, thereby nourishing the relationship and his trust. Think of it: he sent his servant to go and find a wife for his son. And he told him confidently that his God who had told him to leave his family and his country, who had spoken to him and sworn to him to give him the land, would provide the logistical support required for the procurement of a wife for his son.

> The Lord, the God of heaven, who brought me out of my father's household and my native land and who spoke to me and promised me on oath, saying, "To your offspring I will give this land"– he will send his angel before you so that you can get a wife for my son from there (Genesis 24:7).

What a mark of trust! Trust is one of the defining characteristics of friends of God as we shall explore further. Indeed such trust was only possible because he knew God and His ways and because he kept God's dealings on his mind. He remembered God's past faithfulness, and that shaped his image of God.

Our knowledge of God grows as our history with Him grows. And as we think about His works, the consciousness of His goodness and character overwhelm us and we are astounded by His Person. We are awestruck and like Abraham, we fall at His feet. We are emboldened to believe that all will be well in our lives. We are determined to honour Him even as David was when Goliath threatened God's people. He felt the affront deeply. As you think over God's past goodness to you, something happens to you. The desire to please Him grows, and you are captivated by His Person. What He does is a reflection of His character. Properly considered, they create an accurate albeit non-exhaustive picture of Him.

When God took His people out of Egypt, He told Moses that the works He performed were for the purposes of His people knowing Him as God.

> Return to Pharaoh and make your demands again. I have made him and his officials stubborn so I can display my miraculous signs among them. I've also done it so you can tell your children and grandchildren about how I made a mockery of the Egyptians and about the signs I displayed among them—and so you will know that I am the Lord (Exodus 10:1-2).

In teaching this aspect of knowing God, I once gave the people an assignment. They were to go home and in the course of the week, try to remember what God had done for them in the past and make a list of those things. There were several testimonies of how people's perspective of God changed completely after the exercise. They found themselves discovering God's involvement in their lives which had passed unnoticed and they even remembered many divine actions that they had celebrated at one time but quickly forgotten.

All had grown in their knowledge of, and appreciation

of God. Several dimensions of His character had struck them afresh. All were in awe and very eager to share what was for them a most enriching experience. Interestingly, initially many had not seen the point of the exercise but after the first person testified very movingly, the others were subsequently blessed. It led me to think just how much spiritual blessing is missed by believers because of refusal to follow direction from spiritual leadership.

God delights in self-revelation. None can know Him unless He reveals Himself. How privileged we are that He chooses to do so and enables us to be true friends of God.

BOLA OLIVIA OGEDENGBE

2.2

TRUST HIM

Yet he did not waver through unbelief regarding the promise of God, but was strengthened in his faith and gave glory to God, being fully persuaded that God had power to do what he had promised. (Romans 4:20-21)

ONE DAY, A PASTOR FRIEND WAS OVER for lunch. He had previously asked if I would teach in a Bible school he headed and what area would I like to handle. I had said 'faith' as it was something the Lord had dealt with me about many years before. On this occasion, as we spoke, he tried to discourage me from focusing too much on teaching faith since faith teachers had bad press. Before his departure, we had a short time of prayer. Suddenly the Holy Spirit moved on him and he began to prophesy. Strangely, the essence of the prophecy was that the Lord exhorted me to continue to focus on faith, growing in faith and teaching faith, the opposite of the opinion he had expressed so strongly in conversation. It was a humbling and astounding moment. I took the word very much to heart and have endeavoured to stay out of the fray in the religious squabbles about faith, hyper faith, hypo faith we have had over the past few years. Indeed over the years, I have understood why the Lord had been so insistent on my learning to trust Him.

Without that, I doubt that I would have entered into or continued in ministry, such have been the challenges and trials encountered. Nor would I have had the courage, as a single person devoid of alternative income, to step out and trust God to serve Him in full-time ministry—not to talk of the deliverance from sickness and multiple attacks of the devil. None of the breakthroughs I have enjoyed would have happened, nor would any of the healings we have seen in the ministry taken place.

But over and above these things, there is one fundamental advantage of trusting God.

> And the scripture was fulfilled that says, "Abraham believed God, and it was credited to him as righteousness," and he was called God's friend (James 2:23 23).

In this passage, the apostle James establishes the fact of Abraham's faith in God and friendship with God; and one follows on as a consequence of the other. Had Abraham not learnt to trust God, he would not have been as precious to the heart of God as to be called His friend. Without a doubt, trusting God, learning to believe Him is a fundamental characteristic of those who would be friends of God.

The other fundamental characteristic is that of being trusted by God, being a person for whom God can vouch. God said about Abraham:

> Abraham will surely become a great and powerful nation and all nations on earth will be blessed through him (Genesis 18:18).

And yet God Himself had made conditional what He now affirms. It was conditioned by Abraham's obedience. Note verse 19.

> For I have chosen him so that he will direct his children and his household after him to keep the way of the LORD by doing what is right and just so that the LORD will bring about for Abraham what he has promised him (Genesis 18:19).

Could it be that God is sure of his man, that He trusts him to do what is right? But how can God trust a man? I believe the answer to that is because the man trusts and is wholly dependent on Him. God knows that on your own you cannot do or be all He wants. His will can only be done through you if you are dependent on Him since He is the only one who can cause His will to be done. So He will only trust you in the measure that you are submitted to Him and dependent on Him. Therefore dependence on God makes you trustworthy; it assures God that you will be in His camp always, that you will flow with Him and His purposes. It assures Him that He can make plans and include you in them; that you care about what He cares about. Because God is the Source of all, any man who does not trust Him cannot have access to all that is requisite for life; such a man will not be a full fulfiller of divine plans.

Furthermore, the Bible tells us:

> And without faith it is impossible to please God because anyone who comes to him must believe that he exists and that he rewards those who earnestly seek him (Hebrews 11: 6).

A person not pleasing God can hardly be considered His friend. When in the early days of my walk with the Lord, I learned this passage, it was life-changing. I resolved to be a student of God, to learn to please Him, which when you think about it is perfectly reasonable. Can you call a person your friend who distrusts you profoundly, who never believes what you tell them and never expects good from you? You may love them, but you are unlikely to consider them a friend. You tell them it is bright and sunny outside and they proceed to arm themselves with a raincoat.

Take the generation of Abraham's descendants who died in the wilderness. They did so because they did not trust God. These people had been born into slavery and had laboured and suffered atrociously in that estate until their deliverance. They had witnessed every single plague wrought by God to set them free and seen His power working against Egypt and protecting them. They witnessed the plague of flies that covered all of Egypt whereas Goshen, where they lived was spared, according to the word of the Lord through Moses.

> If you do not let my people go, I will send swarms of flies on you and your officials, on your people and into your houses. The houses of the Egyptians will be full of flies; even the ground will be covered with them. "But on that day I will deal differently with the land of Goshen, where my people live; no swarms of flies will be there so that you will know that I, the Lord, am in this land. I will make a distinction between my people and your people. This sign will occur tomorrow," (Exodus 8:21-23).

They also saw the livestock of all Egypt die while theirs was preserved, according to the word of the Lord.

> If you refuse to let them go and continue to hold them back, the hand of the Lord will bring a terrible plague on your livestock in the field–on your horses, donkeys, and camels and on your cattle, sheep, and goats. But the Lord will make a distinction between the livestock of Israel and that of Egypt, so that no animal belonging to the Israelites will die (Exodus 9:2-4).

Pharaoh himself checked afterwards and found it to be so. And when the hail came, it was described as 'the worst storm in the land of Egypt since it had become a nation (Exodus 9:24)', only their region Goshen was spared. Similarly, when the plague of darkness was sent over Egypt, there was light where they lived.

> "So Moses lifted his hand to the sky, and a deep darkness covered the entire land of Egypt for three days. During all that time the people could not see each other, and no one moved. But there was light as usual where the people of Israel lived (Exodus 10:22-23).

These same persons had felt the terror of impending doom as they stood before the Red Sea while Pharaoh's armies closed in on them. They had heaved a sigh of relief and gratefully plunged into the path when God had opened up the Red Sea and made a way through. On the other side, their eyes popping open, they saw the waters close in on Pharaoh and his troops, and joined in Miriam's song of victory. Yet here they were, listening to ten cowardly men sent to spy out the land, tell them it was too hard. Here they were, thinking that men who had not the might of Egypt were too powerful for them.

They strangely did not see that a God who had deployed unusual prowess to rescue them from years of slavery, to humble the power of their oppressor, who had demonstrated supremacy over the elements and sustained them miraculously in the desert was worthy of their trust. They underestimated God's ability to give them victory.

Two men stood out, Joshua and Caleb. Joshua, understandably, but Caleb, from where did he get his confidence? This passage moves me every time I read it. As the people foolishly grumbled against Moses and Aaron and moaned about their lot, these two men were shocked and enjoined them to not rebel against God. Their logic was simple, they remind me of Abraham

- The land is good.
- God will (He is powerful enough to) give us the land if we behave ourselves in a manner that pleases Him.
- We need not be afraid of the people of the land.
- They are now unprotected because God is with us.

In response, the people wanted to stone them. The fulcrum of this passage, for me, is God's perspective of the people's behaviour and faithlessness. He did not only say that they were behaving badly, which they were, that they were cowardly, which they were, He considered it an affront to Himself.

> The Lord said to Moses, "How long will these people treat me with contempt? How long will they refuse to believe in me, in spite of all the signs I have performed among them? (Numbers 14:11).

No, we cannot aspire to be true friends of God unless we determine to trust Him completely. Consequently, it matters to God that we trust Him. Could God have considered Abraham a friend had he not trusted in God's integrity and in God's faithfulness so much so that he was willing to leave his native land to sojourn in a land that would not be his in his own lifetime?

Can you even imagine how pleased God must have been with this man who staked his whole life on the trustworthiness of God without any tangible guarantee? Had he any means of verifying that God would indeed give the land to his descendants? Did he have any means of redress were God to renege on the agreement? What Abraham believed God would do was considerable. It has huge implications for the New Testament believer as there is a consistent correlation drawn between our faith and the faith of Abraham.

What do we mean by trusting God?

Believe He is benevolent and loving towards you

To trust God is to have confidence in His benevolence and love. It is essential that we integrate this concept of divine benevolence. To trust Him is to think good thoughts about Him, to consider that He means well towards you, that all His words, instructions, directions come out of a heart of love and goodness and are intended for your welfare irrespective of the challenges they entail. This is important because sometimes God's instructions rub us the wrong way. We can submit and follow knowing we will not end up at a dead end, with tears of regret or even in a trap. Thus, to trust Him is to consider that He is not an irascible deity whose intentions are suspect. It is to have confidence in the fact that He will never set His own in the path of evil nor visit evil upon them.

To trust Him is to have confidence in His character and in His goodness towards you. He offered good things to Abraham and Abraham believed Him. He visited him once and of all the things you can say to a person, He told him 'I am your shield, your exceedingly great reward'. And Abraham took the cue and said 'what will you give me...?' God Himself is your reward. In Hebrews 11 He affirms that there is a reward for those who pursue a relationship with Him, and we must believe it. Otherwise, we cannot please Him.

> And without faith, it is impossible to please God because anyone who comes to him must believe that he exists and that he rewards those who earnestly seek him (Hebrews 11:6).

Many people feel condemned when they sense a lack of faith in their lives, they think oh, God is not pleased with me. But it may help them to change their perspective of this passage. Rather than focus on their faith or lack thereof why not focus on the promise? See it as a qualifier, not a disqualifier. In other words, the passage affirms the truth that God rewards those who pursue a relationship with Him. So if they will focus on that, which is not that hard, then faith becomes natural. Simply accept that God rewards those who seek Him. And that is it, you are qualified; you please God. In other words, look at the reward, not the problem.

> My prayer has been, Lord, reward me with Yourself, with more knowledge of You, greater intimacy, and more love for You.

There is a reward for being a friend of God. Abraham left hearth and home because he trusted God to do him good. He lived as a wanderer in a foreign land because he had confidence in the God who promised to one day give that land to his descendants; who promised that the nations would be blessed through him; and that his descendants would be more numerous than the sands on the seashore.

Then God stretched out His hand to generations of Abraham's descendants in an offer of friendship they did not always honour. He swore to His good intentions via the prophet as He said

> For I know the plans I have for you, declares the Lord, "plans to prosper you and not to harm you, plans to give you hope and a future," (Jeremiah 29:11).

But they had difficulty believing it. Even today in the church, after many centuries of Scriptural and historical testimony to the goodness of God, there is still an undercurrent of malaise in the hearts of many of God's people. They do not quite see God as a rewarder, as One who is on their side. Consequently, they have a hard time letting go and giving Him the reins of their lives. When you believe that He has good plans for you, then you are willing to receive His plans; you will not thrust your projects on Him.

Believe He has the ability and power to do good

To trust God is to have confidence in His ability and power to act in conformity with the dictates of His goodness and love. In other words, believe that He has the ability to do every good He has promised to do. It is esteeming Him highly as the author and repository of all power. It is honouring Him as Lord over all that exists, every name that is named, considering that all things and circumstances are subject to Him. It is declaring 'Is anything too difficult for God?' As God said to Abraham after Sarah laughed on hearing that she would have a baby.

This is played out in the life of the patriarch in many ways, for instance:

- Abraham dared to believe that a woman of ninety would still have a baby. We know from God's Word that he initially pleaded for Ishmael, but he accepted and trusted that God was able to do this strange thing;
- when the time came, he let go of his son Ishmael because he trusted in God's power to protect him and bless him;
- Abraham was willing to let go of Isaac even though he was the long-awaited child of promise. He believed that God had the capacity, the power to resurrect him. He was confident that God had a plan, and that it was good. Despite the painfulness of the decision, God would do something extraordinary to make things right again.

How sweet our relationship with God becomes when we are able to have such total confidence in Him. Humans are hampered by their inability to change circumstances. God has no such limitations. Beloved, we cannot be distrustful of God. Our hearts must be free towards Him as we embrace His loftiest plans and consider them simple and feasible because of the immense capacity of the author and executor, our God.

Believe He Will Do Good

One day, a leper went to Jesus in need of healing. He fell prostrate before Him and said something that generations of Christians have echoed since.

> Lord, if you are willing, you can make me whole (Matthew 8:2).

He is basically saying, 'Lord I know You can, but do You want to, and will You'? He must have heard of Jesus; he knew He had the power to heal, however, he did not know whether Jesus would use that power on his behalf. So he had no assurance that He would heal him. Believers can be hampered by the same uncertainty. God, they know, is all-powerful but will He exercise the power on their behalf? Possibly not. He is running the universe. He has other fish to fry.

To trust God is to believe that He not only wants, or is able to do us good but that He will so do in line with His promises, His justice, and laws. This is vital because it expresses confidence in His trustworthiness, His willingness, and His honour. You cannot be friends with a person when you doubt their word and their integrity.

Why does this matter? Because what we think of God's character affects the way we relate to Him, what we say to and about Him, thus affecting the depth of our relationship. It also affects the way we respond to Him when we are faced with challenges and even disappointments. Believing that He will do right concerning us gives boldness to trust and obey, to take risks for the sake of the gospel.

That is what Abraham thought despite the vicissitudes of his life. That is why he did not disconnect and return to Haran. And it is for want of this assurance that many Christians think God unfair and draw away. Many do not even want to try trusting God because they are convinced they will be on their own. Others give up in the face of their circumstances which further compounds their distrust.

What about divine sovereignty? Can I dare to trust God blindly when He is sovereign and may or may not decide to do good? God's Word reveals what God in His sovereignty has decided to do. When we meet the conditions on our side, He does what His Word says, in His sovereignty. For instance, He tested Abraham, then He swore from heaven as to what He would do for Abraham because he obeyed. No element of divine sovereignty could have caused Him to unilaterally and unexplainably choose to do otherwise. It would be against His character. The one thing that would void the promise was the non-compliance of the other party, and He made the conditions clear when He made a covenant with Abraham. Abraham met the conditions and God did as He promised. He is a covenant keeping God.

In all ages, He keeps His word. Just as He kept His word to Abraham, He keeps His word to us. The Word of God says:

> Through these he has given us his very great and precious promises, so that through them you may participate in the divine nature, having escaped the corruption in the world caused by evil desires (2 Peter 1:4).

We become partakers of the divine nature. Are these

promises subject to change? No. Will God in His divine sovereignty choose to ignore them? No. He cannot, He will not. It will be a violation of His covenant, and He never violates His covenant.

> The thing to keep in mind about Abraham's faith is that he thought well of God. You cannot be God's friend if you do not think well of Him.

WHY THE DIFFICULTY IN TRUSTING GOD?

A friend of God will consider Him benevolent, good, faithful, able and willing to do right. This will endear him to God and it will affect his own attitude towards the Lord. You are that friend. But why do we find it so hard to trust God? One would think that with the substantial testimony of Scripture as to the goodness of God, trusting Him would come naturally and easily, yet there are factors that militate against a simple childlike faith. We need to identify them so we can mitigate their effect on our lives. Here is a non-exhaustive list of some of these factors (you may want to enter any extra ones you encounter in your life in your prayer journal).

I.   Past negative experience and programming

Who has not had a bad experience with people they trusted who turned out to be unreliable, undependable and sometimes even crooked! People make promises we think binding but which for them are contingent on their mood and willingness. They change their minds unpredictably. Such experiences engender disappointment that if not dealt with can lead to apprehension and negative expectations. Fear of disappointment becomes a mental stronghold.

People are unconsciously programmed to expect the worst to cushion themselves from the potential impact of non-fulfilment. Thus, we continue to hold back, hedge our bets, develop Plan B, just in case. God programmed us to believe, and the world programmes us to disbelieve. That mental attitude is also projected on God. We wonder, doubt, fear, try to hedge our bets. Yet God expects us to trust Him because He is neither fickle nor unreliable. Refusing to trust for fear of disappointment is nonsensical because by not trusting God we are bound to face disappointment and the only way not to be disappointed is to trust Him.

II.   Sin and consciousness of sin

One day a young man spoke to me about one of his co-workers. The man believed in God but was involved in a lifestyle which he knew was sinful. So he was stuck, he could not step out and trust God because he knew he was living a life that did not please God. Many modern teachers will have us believe that it does not matter what we do, so long as we are in Christ, God is pleased with us. That is not so. Sin hinders our faith, not just because we feel guilty but because we are guilty. How can we claim to love and be friends of God when we violate His principles willy-nilly? It is not a friendly thing to do. We may rationalise it all we want, spiritual deadness and apathy is the consequence of sin and people who live in this manner cannot enjoy the freedom of faith.

The other side of this is self-condemnation. When a person is walking right before God but is consistently condemning his or herself, that person is not trusting in the cleansing power of the blood of Jesus over their life. So they sense a continual discomfort in their relationship with God and cannot please Him totally. When we live without a revelation of God's righteousness afforded to us in the new birth, we lack the confidence to come boldly to God. Some believe that they are not important and even if God was going around dispensing gifts, He would not stop at their door. They believe they are mere miserable, wretched sinners. And their wrong thinking about God hinders their intimacy with God and trust in God.

III.   Low level of experience with God

Do you remember when David went to the battlefield to take victuals to his brothers? He found the soldiers, grown men all, king included, cowering before the champion of the Philistines. He on the other hand, boldly affirmed that he could take the man out since he had defied the armies of God. What gave him such confidence? His track record with God. He remembered past situations where God had enabled him to slay vicious opponents and said this one too shall know the same fate. Do you have a history with God? Do you have a record of God's dealings with you? Do they inspire you to trust Him yet again?

Notice the confidence of Abraham when he sent his servant to find a wife for his son. He told him to not take a wife for his son among the inhabitants of the land where he lived, but to go back to his own people to find him a wife. The man understandably expressed concern that the woman may not want to return with him, upon which Abraham said this

> The LORD, the God of heaven, who brought me out of my father's household and my native land and who spoke to me and promised me on oath, saying, 'To your offspring I will give this land' — he will send his angel before you so that you can get a wife for my son from there (Genesis 24:7).

He had an understanding of God's character, God's identity, God's covenant with him and a record of God's past dealings with him. On the basis of that, he chose the more difficult path in the matter of his son's marriage, believing, that God would intervene supernaturally. This is a man conscious of being on a mission for God, and conscious that what concerns him concerns God. This is a far cry from the Abraham who pretended his wife was not his wife to save his neck. This is a man who has the audacity to believe that the God of heaven would care who his son marries and would dispatch an angel from heaven to ensure the whole matter is settled the right way.

You also have a covenant with God. To you also He has made great promises. Do you believe that God cares enough about you to dispatch His angels to settle matters for you? Will you step up and start trusting Him or will you go for the path of least resistance? You can begin your own history with God today. Even if you have not been in the habit of stepping out in faith and leaning on Him at all times, you have this one thing, the experience of salvation.

You stepped out then and believed God. That was the hardest thing for you to do, entrust your eternal salvation into the hands of an invisible God. Now that it is done, you can now live by faith, trusting the same God on a day-to-day basis. Keep a record of God's wonderful dealings with you, they will encourage you.

IV.   Lack of knowledge of God

Many do not trust Him because they have but scant knowledge of Him and His Word. They have entered the gate in the new birth and now they play near the entrance. They have not ventured further in to discover the riches of kingdom life, so God remains distant to them. It is indifference masquerading as reverence.

Prayer, Scripture meditation and study are not duties undertaken to please God. They are not activities with any inherent value which only serve to demonstrate our obedience and seriousness. Neither is their activities undertaken to humour God who for whatever reason seems to get some kick out of it. This is God's appointed way of making Himself known to us. We neglect them at our peril. Indeed, negligence in this area is one of the causes of the low level of revelation and knowledge of God and His Word in the church. Without them, no one can have a rich, full and satisfying fellowship with God. Every day, seek to know God better. That is the purpose of our existence.

V. The pressure of present circumstances

Have you ever sat down and felt thoroughly overwhelmed by events around you? Perhaps you even opted to go to sleep to avoid having to deal with anything. That is another reason why people have difficulty in trusting God, they are submerged by the pressure of their circumstances. Fear can also bind itself around your heart until you live constantly with a sense of dread. You awake in the morning thinking you are about to sink. At those moments, you are more likely to complain than trust. But that is precisely the time to stare down the circumstances and say as Paul said in the midst of the storm, I know the One in whom I have believed. Jesus in the parable of the sower, warned us against the negative effect of the cares, worries, and pressures of the world on our ability to retain the Word of God.

Yes, pressure can get to people and blind them from trusting God. It happened to the descendants of Jacob in Egypt after Pharaoh had increased their burden as a result of Moses calling on him to let them go. The people were very upset. The Lord spoke to Moses and made some astounding promises which Moses relayed to them. He said that He would move mightily against Pharaoh and that Pharaoh would end up driving the people out of his country. He identified Himself yet again and recalled His covenant to give them the land where they had lived as foreigners. He mandated Moses to tell the people that

1. He would deliver them from slavery with mighty acts of judgement,

2. He would make them His own people and be their God,

3. He would bring them into the land He had sworn to give to their forefathers and

4. He would give them the land.

> Moses reported this to the Israelites, but they did not listen to him because of their discouragement and harsh labour (Exodus 6:9).

They did not listen to God, but they listened to the devil and their flesh. They listened to Pharaoh and his retaliatory tactics. They listened to the pressure of their circumstances. What a response to such a mighty promise! We need to be on our guard so that discouragement will not kill discernment.

VI. Delay

Yet another factor that impairs our intimacy with God is delayed manifestation. It can shake a person's confidence and cause them to become ambivalent about God. In the book of Malachi, it speaks of the complaints of God's people as they see the wicked prosper while the righteous apparently suffered. The same temptations beset us all. But we can consider Abraham and 'look to the rock from which we were hewn'.

I imagine the patriarch must have had moments when he meditated on his unfortunate circumstances as year after year nothing seemed to change. When God came back to visit with him, God told him not to fear, that He was his shield, in other words, He would protect and care for him; and that He would reward him abundantly. This was all good, but Abraham had one concern and I love the way the New Living Translation puts it.

> But Abram replied, "O Sovereign Lord, what good are all your blessings when I don't even have a son? Since you've given me no children, Eliezer of Damascus, a servant in my household, will inherit all my wealth. You have given me no descendants of my own, so one of my servants will be my heir." (Genesis 15:2-3).

God's answer was that it would not be so. Despite the delay, the promise would come to pass. He would have the promised child. The end would be good. And it most certainly was. God said something similar to His people through the prophet Malachi. He promised to honour those who, despite the circumstances continued to speak well of Him. We will deal with this some more in the chapter on honouring God.

VII. Demonic attacks

Sometimes the pressure is not just from your circumstances; it is from the devil endeavouring to paint bleak pictures of your future as though there was no way out. But there is a way out. With God, there is always a way out. Spirits of discouragement attack people and they see everything in a negative light. Hope seems far away and again, their first reaction is to complain that God is not doing His job in their lives.

Every factor, circumstance, or situation that makes us fearful, distrustful and suspicious of God and His dealings with us is suspect. If left unchecked, it will bring separation and hinder our friendship with God. Remember, the measure of your friendship is the measure of your thinking about God.

How do I develop my trust in God?

Decide

Our eternal destiny hinged on a decision, to accept God's offer and work of salvation in Christ. Our continual walk of faith and intimacy with God hinges on a decision; we must choose to live a life of faith. It does not just happen. As we have seen previously, life happens to us and brings in its wake a cortege of factors and circumstances that sap faith, neuter strength and erode intimacy. Make the decision today. Declare 'I will develop my trust in God.

I will not fold my hands passively or pontificate on theology while my soul is withering for lack of divine friendship. I will not be a dilettante. I will not flip aimlessly and purposelessly through the Word. I will be a powerful believer, like Abraham, 'strong in faith'. I will make a conscious decision to grow in trust. I will conscientiously build my faith'. When you have made the decision, then begin to apply the other principles in this section. I guarantee you, in less time than you imagine, your heart will become more established in God and your love for Him will deepen.

Seek revelation knowledge of God

We trust as far as we know. As we saw in the chapter on knowing God, the believer's primary pursuit must be to know God as much as God desires to be known. And the primary way by which He enables us to know Him is through His Word. Treat it as important and give it time. Seek out revelation. Ten minutes in the Word of God per day will not make you a giant of faith. When we seek, we are saying to God, my relationship with You matters to me. A low level of intimacy with God is a reflection of human desire, not God's, of human efforts, not God's.

Understand divine desire, plans, promises – become addicted to the voice of God

Some people are inscrutable. Some appear to be what they are not. There is no art, King Duncan rightly said, to find the mind's construction in the face. When you do not know where a person is going, what they are thinking, what they want, you cannot entrust yourself to them. Some people are taking their chances with God. They see Him as inscrutable, but they are trying very hard to trust Him hoping everything will turn out well. That is no recipe for friendship.

The very existence of the Bible is proof that God does not want to keep His plans and actions to Himself. He loves to share. Look at Abraham, God told him what His plans for him were; look at Moses, God told him what He wanted to do for the Israelites; look at Paul, God told him what He wanted to do with his life.

Seek to gain an understanding of God's heart, God's

desires, plans, and promises. As your understanding increases, your trust grows. You are reassured, encouraged and prepared.

CHOOSE TO BELIEVE

We come to many crossroads in faith. There we choose to believe or disbelieve. We sometimes feel as if we were standing on the edge of a precipice and if God does not hold out His hand, we will plunge into the abyss. Those are the moments that make or mar a man. At that point, we make a choice to panic or to pray, to fear or to be in faith. What do we do? We pray, we stand in faith, we deliberately choose to praise God for His intervention rather than bemoan His non-intervention.

A few Cassandras will consider it their Christian duty to point out the facts and prove you are being unrealistic. Just choose to believe that God has the ability to make things happen irrespective of the circumstances. Their predecessors thought Jesus was unrealistic when He told Jairus to believe and not fear after Jairus was informed of his daughter's death. They thought He was being unrealistic when He told Peter to take the boat out again to fish even though Peter had already fished all night and caught nothing. No doubt had they known they would have thought Abraham unrealistic when he reasoned that God could bring Isaac back to life.

KILL THE BEAR

What? A bear? Yes. When David was a shepherd and a bear would come to devour his sheep, he would attack it and kill it. He did the same with lions. Little did he know that it was his training ground for the encounter that would make him a national hero and push him into his destiny, the besting of Goliath the giant. Had he run when faced with the bear, he would not have developed the courage, capacity, and confidence to face down the boasting giant.

Every one of us has their own bears. Identify yours and tackle them. Take the small steps today that build your faith in God. Trust God in the challenges. Trust Him daily in the simple things, in fellowship through the day. It seemed like a big deal for Abraham to trust God to have a son at 100, but he did. And it prepared him to be able to give up that son to God and trust God to bring him back to life.

> Your current level of intimacy with God is a reflection of your desire, not God's, of your efforts, not God's.

Benefits of trusting God

As we have reiterated, trusting God is essential to friendship with God. A man who will be God's friend must believe that He is, and that He rewards those who seek Him. Here are some other attendant benefits of trusting God. When you trust

- You will be free from worry.
- You will have a vibrant prayer life and deep enjoyment of the Word of God.
- Others will trust God because of you. Abraham's

servant believed God would intervene and help him on his mission because of God's past faithfulness to Abraham.

- You will be strong. Faith makes you powerful and unshakeable. You become victorious and join the ranks of those who cause demons to tremble.

It delights the heart of God that in adverse circumstances, we continue to trust Him.

Can God trust you?

God trusted Abraham, not because he was perfect, but because he trusted God and consequently was obedient, and passed the test. God wants to trust us and He will when we trust Him. Trust is dependence; dependence on God makes you trustworthy. It shows that you are and will stay in God's camp. When a person is totally dependent and in tune with God, God can easily include them in His plans because they care about what He cares about.

Not only that, God can be certain that they will fulfil His purposes. Why? Because they are leaning on the One who is the Source of all. So God can trust a person who trusts God because a person who trusts God has access to all of God's resources to fulfil a divine purpose. Without Him, we can do nothing. Staying in the vine is the only way that the branches can bear fruit. God knows that on your own you cannot do all that He wants. His will can only be done through you if you are dependent on Him since He is the only one who makes it happen. Any man who does not trust Him cannot have access to all that is requisite for life; such a man will not be a full fulfiller of divine plans. So He will only trust you in the measure that you are submitted to Him and dependent on Him.

Let us aspire to a life greater than what we have today. We are not rats who must scramble for crumbs to live on. We are creatures made in the image of God; we have received the life of God and are called to be friends of God. Let us devote our lives to that. All other things, Jesus promises, will be added to us.

2.3

AGREE WITH HIM

Can two walk together, except they be agreed? (Amos 3:3).

MANY YEARS AGO, AS A POSTGRADUATE STUDENT in Paris, a friend insisted on introducing me to another student of his acquaintance. He was convinced we would be great friends. We liked each other on sight; however, we were extremely dissimilar. It would seem that we only had one thing in common, our deep-seated love for God. We both felt this was a divine friendship; however, our differences in temperament, style, etc were major enough to apparently preclude any form of closeness. We had endless disagreements and misunderstandings. We did not seem to see eye to eye on anything, so much so that both of us went to the Lord about it in frustration.

We understood from Amos 3:3 that we had a choice, a choice to agree to walk together, to meet and enrich each other's lives and to serve God together. Gradually, we ironed out the differences and ended up being close friends despite our differing styles. In agreeing to walk together in the Lord, we found harmony and agreement in the walk.

The Importance of Harmony

Harmony is essential in any relationship. It is possible for our relationship with God to lack harmony and agreement. Indeed one outcome or trigger of the fall is that man chose to disagree with God, then began to think differently from God and as a result, veered completely off track. He could no longer walk in intimacy with God. He lost sensitivity to divine ways and his thinking became perverted. It became twisted and distorted, alien to divine logic. Our ideas of good and evil differ from His, our opinions on direction and actions do not tally with His. So we pray, but there is something else that needs to occur over and above, as well as through prayer. It is a moulding of our desires to conform to God's.

Let's make this simple. Think of two people sharing a flat who cannot agree on anything. They disagree on the right indoor temperature in winter, on playing music at night and even on the fact that one wants to do night vigils praying loudly in tongues while the other wants to sleep. We know that flatmates need to live in harmony, that disagreement will jeopardise the harmony in the home.

Why do we think we can be in disagreement with God and yet be close to Him? What would it be like if you had a friend and when you wanted to take the bus, they said no, let's take the train? You finally say 'ok, the train it is, here's a blue one.' Then, it is 'oh no I prefer the red one'. Then it is 'Let's walk on the right side of the road', 'No, I prefer the left'. You serve them red meat and they cannot stand the sight of it, they only eat vegetables. You peel a banana, and they cannot sit in the room with a person eating a banana because they are chronically allergic to it. None of these are absolutes, only preferences; not even the banana allergy.

Now imagine when there are absolutes, when God who is the Author of truth, life, and all substance says which is the way to go, and we, well we, do not quite see it that way. Some will even say the preacher should not say it is that way as it bothers them. The unavowed inference is the idea that human thinking is the best, that God's ways are good but nonessential or perhaps even impractical. No matter how many proverbs and aphorisms exist in different cultures about the folly of mankind, it is a folly that we still hold strongly to. It makes sense to us. And it makes a mess of our spiritual lives.

We erroneously believe we are in agreement with God when we praise and thank Him for a blessing or a victory in our lives. Temporary gratitude is not concord, it is certainly not agreement. We demonstrate our agreement and harmony with God when we are faced with a challenge or an instruction—when something is required of us, not when something is given to us.

For instance, there are people whose relationship with

God bears a strong pecuniary and mercantile component. It is always about God giving something material or tangible. Such people will often find themselves in contention with God over what they perceive as 'unanswered prayer'. 'God, what are you doing?' 'God, why have you not done this or that'? 'Are you sure you love me, I don't have a job, this sister here is not as consecrated as I am and she has a good job?' It is an endless refrain of lamentation and jibes; anything save harmonious. But when your relationship with God is based on an exchange of love, not things, you will never find it wanting. Besides, God is not responsible for any shortcomings in our lives, we and the devil are.

We are destined to harmony. God has agreed to walk with us; we must agree to walk with Him. And we must choose to walk in agreement. He makes Himself available to us; we make ourselves submissive to Him. God resists the proud, that we know. So we attain agreement; not agreement of the kind I had with my friend, but one of a higher kind, where we embrace His thoughts willingly. You cannot be friends with God if you refuse to think like Him because He does not express opinions, He expresses truth. So the onus is on man to adapt to God, not the other way round. But that is the hard part. Why?

- Because our way makes sense to us. The ways of God are alien to us, and we may chafe at His practices and principles. That is why many people spend their lives arguing with and against God, subject to conflicting emotions about the choices incumbent on their faith.

- Because, as said earlier, some see God's ways as impracticable and opt to do things their way while still professing to love God.

- Because of fear. When God sets aside His own natural laws in order to demonstrate His power, we quake at the thought that it just might not work.
- Because circumstances conspire to frustrate our expectations. Too many disappointments, too much delay and we conclude it could not have been so, to begin with.
- Because we agree with the people who disagree with God.
- Because we are not captivated by the mind of God. God wants people who are willing to think like Him.

Examples to Follow - Walk in Their Footsteps

Everything God requires us to do, someone before us has done it successfully. We can and should follow in their footsteps.

Abraham agreed with God

What shall we say in this regard about Abraham? As we look at the life of the principal character of our study, we notice Abraham's obedience; but his obedience was founded on his agreement. Often we try to obey without agreeing and it only makes obedience burdensome. When God spoke to Abraham and called him out of Haran after the death of his father, he had to agree that God's way was right and that his destiny was different from all that he had ever known or believed. He agreed to walk with God and embrace divine perspective. When he came into the land, he arrived in Shechem by the oaks of Mamre, and his eyes met a spectacle that did not conform to the grand ideas of him possessing the land. It is said that the Canaanites were in the land. They were well entrenched and well established, but Abraham did not go back where he came from. He lived as a 'wandering Aramean'.

God never ceased communicating His heart to Abraham. As we have seen, He constantly reiterated His promise to Abraham in order that he might keep seeing the same thing as God. Once, as recounted in Genesis 15, Abraham received a vision from the Lord. In the vision, God reassured Abraham (still Abram) of His protection and provision. As we saw earlier, Abraham complained of his continuing childlessness and the possibility that a servant would be his heir. God said not so.

> Then the word of the Lord came to him: "This man will not be your heir, but a son who is your own flesh and blood will be your heir. He took him outside and said, "Look up at the sky and count the stars—if indeed you can count them." Then he said to him, "So shall your offspring be." Abram believed the Lord, and he credited it to him as righteousness (Genesis 15.4-6).

Do you see what is happening here? Abraham is expected to agree to God's plan to give him a child. To help him out, God gives him a graphic display of what his offspring will be like. The sight of the stars helped to establish and renew in Abraham's mind and heart the truth of what he had been told, thereby securing his acquiescence. The consequence of that was that he believed. Agreeing with God and with His plans is sometimes the missing link in our endeavours of faith.

Abraham agreed he would be a father and that Eliezer would not be his heir.

So that's that for the child but he still needed to know for sure about the land. Can you give me confirmation, he requested? No problem, God replied and proceeded to make a covenant with him; using the traditions to which he was accustomed. He had him present three 3-year-old animals as well as a dove and a pigeon. Abraham agreed. He cut the animals in two. He placed the halves opposite each other on the ground along with the whole birds. They were symbols of the covenant to be concluded. He had to keep away the birds of prey as the elements must be untouched and unmutilated. Then a lengthy wait till sundown ensued for God to show up. I cannot help wondering how long we would have waited, and whether we would have troubled ourselves to do what God asked us to do.

God put Abraham to sleep and revealed to him his own future as well as the four hundred year sojourn of his descendants in a foreign land, their future bondage and subsequent release with great wealth. They would return to the land God had promised Abraham, at which point the current inhabitants would be judged for their sins. It was a most extraordinary encounter. At sundown, a smoking torch and flaming oven went between the pieces; God thereby made an irrevocable covenant with Abraham. A legally binding agreement was signed on untearable paper with indelible ink that God would do all that He had promised to do. He solemnly pledged to give them the land and specifically named the people who would cede the land to them. Abraham could be in no doubt that God meant business. Yet another picture was imprinted on Abraham's mind, one that he could think on and be reminded of God's commitment to him.

To agree with God is to recognise that His ways are best and to consider that His decisions in every situation are the only option possible. That is what we witness in the life of the patriarch when he found himself instructed by God to send away Ishmael his teenage son. For over a decade he had seen this boy as the fulfilment of God's promise to him and all his hopes rested on the lad. God had spoken about Isaac again and insisted it was through Isaac that the promise would be fulfilled. Fine enough, but give up the elder? Were you to be in Abraham's shoes, would you really have seen the point of letting go of a teenager to focus all your attention and hopes on a baby?

I once heard someone preach that Isaac was born to Sarah at the time when she finally believed. Their point was that the only reason Abraham waited was because Sarah had not believed before. Then they went on to say that God does not test people because He is a good God. And yet we are told that God decided to test Abraham by asking him to give up his son Isaac. And the wonder of it is that Abraham agreed with God. Why? He had started thinking like God.

The beauty of this passage is in seeing the astounding progression in Abraham's mindset. It did not appear illogical to him, he did not have difficulty seeing God's point. His thinking had so changed that God's Word tells us that he thought God was able to raise Isaac from the dead. And since he thought that, he obviously thought also that this was not the end of the story as God had made a promise that was bound to be fulfilled. Perhaps, he realised it was a test; perhaps he simply thought that God certainly had a good reason for requiring it of him. And that is where we must get to if we want to live in harmony with God. We must hear God's instructions, see God's laws and conclude that He has good reason for wanting it so, and so it should be indeed, and so we will do. We cannot be second-guessing Him, disagreeing with His principles, countering His instructions and imagine that friendship and intimacy will be unhindered.

JESUS AGREED WITH THE FATHER

Jesus demonstrated for us what life would look like were we to be in perfect harmony with the Father. He was. He saw what the Father was doing and agreed with it, He heard what the Father was saying and agreed with it. Consequently, He reproduced the same thing. He, in essence, put Himself forward as One who was wholly dependent on the Father to function, who did what the Father did and said only what the Father said, only. And in the garden of Gethsemane when in His humanity He would rather have stepped away from the horrors of the sacrifice, He chose to agree with the Father's desire, saying 'Not my will, but yours'. In other words, despite the pressure and the burden of the moment, I accept that Your way is best. I choose to agree with You.

He is our example. In coming to the earth, He willingly subordinated Himself to the Father and took on a humble role. We are enjoined to think like Him. One self-styled 'Grace' preacher said, to prove the point that God is always pleased with us irrespective of our conduct, that God was pleased with Jesus at His baptism even though He had as yet done nothing. I listened in stunned surprise. The incarnation was nothing? Renouncing equality with God to take on the form of a servant was nothing? The Creator reduced to taking the form of His creation was nothing? No, it was an act of utmost submission, humility, and agreement.

How do you live in agreement with God?

Acknowledge that His way is perfect

> As for God, His way is perfect, the word of the Lord is tested and true (Psalm 18.30).

As mentioned earlier, one of the causes of discord among people is the refusal to acknowledge the rightness of the other person's ways. And our relationship with God is no exception. This means that we begin the move towards harmony with God by recognising that all His thoughts, plans and ways are just and perfect. It is a simple shift, but an essential one. We will not even commence the process of the renewal of the mind unless we are completely convinced that His way is perfect. Now tell me, when you see what is perfect, and it is at your disposal, will you not run to embrace it? Not only is His way perfect, but His Word has proven its reliability and truthfulness. It has been tested, and it still proves true. It has not been and can never be found wanting.

Taking such a stand is increasingly difficult in our age because of the many attacks against the authenticity and even morality of Scripture. We must crave revelation so that truth will be evident to us and we will continue to honour God's Word and ways as perfect. We cannot despise His Word and revere Him. So settle in your mind, that God's ideas and plans are true, real and effective.

BELIEVE THAT HIS WAYS ARE HIGHER THAN YOURS

Alongside his thoughts, our ideas, grand though they may be, pale into insignificance. Abraham was no fool; he had ideas for his life before God revealed Himself to him. However, he had the good sense, despite his limitations, to understand that this was thinking on a scale higher than any he could aspire to.

In Isaiah 55, God puts us in our place. He makes it clear that we must acknowledge the superiority of His thoughts and ways over ours. We are wise when we recognise that He knows things of which we are in the dark, can predict the end of a thing that is yet to commence; and that we have no means of penetrating His wisdom unless He graciously grants us access. We are often proud of our knowledge and our science, but that is only because we are ignorant of the depths of knowledge still unfathomable to us. We are like children who boast about reading through a ten-page picture book to a scholar who has worked on hundreds of encyclopaedias.

To get the point home to us, God uses a striking simile to show just how different and puny our thinking is compared to His. He says the gap between His thinking and ours is akin to that between the heavens and the earth.

Ponder it and then ask yourself if you want these higher thoughts to rule your life or your own lower thoughts.

> "For my thoughts are not your thoughts, neither are your ways my ways," declares the Lord. "As the heavens are higher than the earth, so are my ways higher than your ways and my thoughts than your thoughts." (Isaiah 55:8-9).

So it begins with surrender. It begins with you giving Him a blank cheque to help you change your mind.

Accept that His ways are normal and valid for you

I may agree that God's way is perfect, that His way is higher than mine, but still insist that His way is His way because He is God, and my way is valid for me because I am human. In fact, 'I am only human' is an often-heard explanation for subtle compromises and outright disobedience in the church. The idea is prevalent that God's ways are not practicable for a normal human being. We must agree that his ways are normative for us or we jeopardise intimacy. God is seeking our agreement more than our perfection. What hinders us is more the stubborn resistance to accepting God's ways than the failings of the flesh.

So we agree to change our perspective of normalcy. Let me give you an example. For the disciples of Jesus, to cross the river by boat is normal. For Jesus, to walk on the water is normal. For the disciples, to consider that you need a year's wages to feed thousands of people is normal; for Jesus, to use a handful of fish and bread for the same purpose is normal. For the disciples, to work hard to earn a salary to pay taxes is normal, for Jesus, to get the money out of the mouth of a fish is normal. And in each case Jesus expected them to adopt His way, they did, and it worked. You might say Peter almost drowned, but it was not because he walked on the water, rather because he feared the waves. Jesus did not say to him 'why did you walk on the water?' He said 'why did you doubt'?

One of the reasons why we fail in faith is that we struggle to believe something that we find patently absurd or impossible for a human being, so our mind fights us relentlessly. Sarah laughed when she heard she would bear a child. The absurdity of it all hit her. She was expected to feel sexual desire at her age and have intercourse with her husband; she would then conceive, which she had been unable to do even as a young woman.

But, as God rightly said, is anything too hard for God? She came to see the truth of it and found her place in the hall of fame of faith heroes in Hebrews 11. This is an invitation to an extraordinary life. God wants to elevate our thinking beyond the natural order of things for unredeemed men. Christians ought to be the most adventurous people on earth, crossing oceans in our minds, besting giants and subduing evil.

TRAIN YOURSELF TO KNOW AND ACCEPT HIS WAYS

Once you have acknowledged the perfection, excellence, and normalcy of His ways, the next step is to devote the rest of your existence to pursuing the knowledge of His will and His ways; and, bringing your own thinking into line with His. Theology must lead to transformation.

Consequently, the apostle Paul after a lengthy exposition of redemption, faith, and salvation continues his letter to the Romans by saying

> Do not conform to the pattern of this world, but be transformed by the renewing of your mind. Then you will be able to test and approve what God's will is — his good, pleasing and perfect will (Romans 12:2).

We are enjoined to renounce the ways of this world and to change our minds. Remember, to agree with God is to agree with His thinking concerning His principles, His promises, His plans, and His actions; all that is revealed to us, we are expected to acquiesce. Here are a few suggestions as to how you can train yourself in this regard.

I.   Choose your 'shaper'

The word 'conform' is the Greek word, 'suschematizesthai'; its root is schema and refers to the outward form that varies from year to year. The 'Bible du Semeur' translation says 'do not allow yourself to be shaped by this world'. Do you get the picture? Back in the 80s in London, England, people who had adopted the punk lifestyle used to hang out on Oxford Street and in the environs. Being a foreigner I found them very striking, they were different from the rest of society, they did not allow society to fashion them, however, they conformed to one another. Someone is fashioning you.

Our environment, family, society, and education have shaped us and that affects our attitude towards God.

God is saying that we should no longer allow that to happen. We are the clay and He, not anyone else, is the potter. Yet God has made us beings with a will, and we must choose to yield our will to Him. No one lives in a vacuum. Something and/or someone is shaping your life and thinking other than God. So we must choose to distance ourselves from the mindset of our generation that is opposed to God, rather than judge God's thinking on the basis of the mindset of our generation.

Every believer must choose to no longer fashion their cloth after this pattern. Nor must they keep trying to merge God's pattern with that of the world. Can one craft a splendid garment by piecing together two dissimilar sewing patterns with conflicting measurements and styles? No, never the twain shall meet. So your old manner of thinking is a hindrance to you knowing what is good, pleasing and perfect to God.

II. Focus on God as the shaper and changer

We come into harmony with God by thinking like God. To think like God, we deliberately choose to change the way we think to reflect the way He thinks. We allow Him to shape our thoughts, perspectives, vision, and world. And that process leads to change. Here it is, God calls it the 'renewal of the mind'. Renewal is 'anakainosis'. In Greek, there are two words for new—neos and kainos. Neos means new from a temporal perspective, kainos means new in terms of character and nature. Renewal of the mind thus is changing your thinking patterns, attitude, thoughts, and perspective. That is what God sought to do with Abraham when He showed him the stars as a picture of his future offspring. His thinking began to change, and he could agree with God that he would become a father and not remain a childless man.

It is as our minds are made new that we will have the right understanding and approach to God's plans and principles. We are thus empowered to more fully apprehend what God's will is. Accurate perception and acceptance of the will of God is predicated upon an altered mindset. Mental acceptance has had a very bad press because it is often substituted for heart faith. That being so, we still need to recognise the rightness, authority, and superiority of God's thoughts and adopt them. Our Father wants us to willingly undergo a transformation, a metamorphosis, from the Greek word 'metamorphousthai'. This transformation is the inevitable consequence of coming into agreement with God in our mind.

So choose to engage the process of change whereby your thinking changes to reflect God's perspective. It is in so doing that you will know what God wants, wills, and desires. God wants you to have a mind in harmony with His mind, free from captivity to Satan, to the world and to the flesh; a mind that reflects the mind of Christ. God sent Philip out to the road to Gaza and he simply said OK and went, zero resistance to God's will. That is the way to be. Practice saying Yes Lord and following through. You may get to take Air Heaven on your way back too.

III.   God's Word is an agent of transformation

God gave Joshua an astounding master key to harmony with God and success in every area of life, His Word. Picture this, the great Moses had passed on. The burden of taking the people to the Promised Land fell on his assistant Joshua, a military man. He needed more than military might to direct these people who had proved to be quite a challenge for Moses himself. He had witnessed the challenges to Moses's leadership, the loss of an entire generation in the wilderness because of unbelief and rebellion. Now the onus was on him to do what Moses had not finished. It was a daunting task.

> Keep this Book of the Law always on your lips; meditate on it day and night, so that you may be careful to do everything written in it. Then you will be prosperous and successful. (Joshua 1:8)

Do you see the connection with Romans 12? Meditating day and night on God's Word will produce insight, understanding, clarity, a change of mindset, and faith. Add obedience to the mix, and the outcome will be continual success. Simply put, consider, agree, obey and you will succeed. The next chapter covers obedience, but what we see here is that knowing and accepting God's way precedes the doing of it. It seems to me that God wants to soak our brains in His Word. Whatever you meditate on extensively will condition your thinking.

Meditating day and night on the Word empowers you to think like God and relate to Him in a meeting of minds. Some will say it is a no-brainer of course. The mind of God is revealed in His Word. To agree with Him, we do not need to hear voices in the night, we need to submit to His Word. It was given to teach and train us in righteousness. And you will find that the more time you spend thinking on God's Word and ways, the greater your intimacy and consciousness of God will be.

IV. Develop a willing attitude

Let me challenge you to position yourself as a friend of God. A friend of God thinks like God. The Scriptures say that friendship with the world is enmity with God. Holding on to the thinking of our age is being a friend of the world and an enemy of God. Many believers have the same attitude towards the church as non-Christians do; they treat it as this antiquated structure that is out of tune with its age. They lampoon those Christians who hold on to God's standards and ways as being 'conservative'. They are the ones who have sold out to a godless generation and jeopardised their intimacy with God. Choose otherwise. Remember, His way is perfect; His Word is tested and true.

The Lord taught me many years ago to pray this 'Lord, I give you a blank cheque', and 'Lord, I give you Carte Blanche'. Trust God to work things out according to the counsel of His will. You do not want to be one of those who say 'I am a Christian but....' And proceed to say something that violates God's Word.

Think of Moses, God had him born in the heat of the persecution of Hebrew male children. Not only did He save him, He made the Egyptians themselves raise him and care for him. Moses felt a call but was out of tune with God, he got into trouble and left. Forty years later, God goes to get him, this time he walks in tandem with God, follows His every instruction and he brings down the power of Egypt without a sword. God had found His man who would listen to Him. He spoke to Moses face to face. In Abraham, He found a man who was willing to listen and accept His way of doing things. I pray He will find such a man or woman in you.

Conclusion

Receiving and adopting divine perspective must be the bedrock of our lives. Man must seek to know God's mind and agree with it. Agreement may include understanding but not necessarily. God's ways surpass ours, His mind is beyond ours. However, we can make the decision to submit to His thinking and consider a thing to be so because He says it. So as a lifestyle seek to ascertain His will and agree with it. Then take action to align yourself with it; that is obedience and the subject of the next chapter.

BOLA OLIVIA OGEDENGBE

2.4

OBEY HIM

You are my friends if you do what I command (John 15:14).

AS WE EXPLORE THE LIFESTYLE OF A man or woman who would be a true friend to God, let us remember that our object is not merely to say that God is our friend. We have seen, in Book 1 the extraordinary benefits that we derive from the relationship. Our focus now is on the benefits, were that to be possible, that God would derive from His friendship with us. Our goal then is that we also become people who God can consider as His friends. We aim to be persons who care not only for their interest but for the interest of the Master, those who will acquiesce to all His desires because it fulfils His purpose.

Our age is one in which men seek convenience at the expense of truth, they seek reassurance rather than reality. In such an age we fashion golden calves that we carry, who do our bidding and we call them Elohim. In the past they were fashioned with wood and stone; now we fashion them with our minds and imagination, we portray them eloquently with our tongues. These idols are mute, they cannot speak; we are their voice. They cannot express opinions contrary to ours, they cannot demand obedience. We put in their mouths what we will and we call it a 'thus sayeth the Lord'. Thus is our age.

And yet we are called to friendship with the Living God who can speak, a sovereign Being who can lay down conditions for intimacy. The book of Hebrews tells us that in sundry times in the past, God spoke through the prophets but now in these last days, He has spoken through the Son. The Son spoke to His disciples and to us and laid down this one requirement for being considered by Him as a friend.

> You are my friends if you do what I command you (John 15:14).

In other words, you are my friends 'if you obey me'. Clearly, obedience is a prerequisite for deep friendship with God.

WHAT DO WE MEAN BY 'OBEYING GOD?'

Submission and obedience to God are the corollaries of mutual submission in friendship. Obedience is my expression of my agreement and the manifestation of my loyalty. It is indispensable to harmony. Obedience is expressing my conviction that God's way is the right way, that God's thoughts are the right thoughts, that God's instructions are right. It is recognising God's authority and right to order His universe, orchestrate our affairs and direct my steps. Obedience is bowing to His superiority in wisdom and understanding. It is a demonstration of my faith in His Person, a manifestation of my submission and a work of grace. Obedience is a natural consequence of salvation and the purpose of salvation. We are saved to obey.

To obey is to do what you know God wants you to do, irrespective of the circumstances or the cost. What He wants, when He wants, the way He wants.

1. To obey is to follow His written Word. God's Word shows what is right; it gives us a picture of holiness.

2. It is to follow God's instructions and vision for your life, follow the grand plan, day-to-day instructions, and promptings of the Spirit.

3. To obey is to follow God's direction for your community of faith.

4. It is to do the things that advance the kingdom of God.

5. It is to examine each thought, word and action to see whether or not they draw us nearer to God.

The obedience of Abraham

God said about Abraham, he is 'my friend'. God found in him a man who heard Him, who agreed with Him and who did what He told him to do. Abraham's life was marked by a spectacular degree of obedience, of which we find some instances below

Leaving his home

We have no record of anyone in Abraham's general environment in Ur or Haran who was a devoted follower of God nor do we have any testimonies of those who followed God before him and who encouraged him to 'trust the Lord', 'he will see you through'. Yet he chose to do what God said. When we think of how essential the obedience of this one man was to God's plan of salvation for mankind, we cannot but be grateful that he was such as to follow God.

One cannot but desire to walk in his footsteps and go beyond the call of duty to leave a legacy of faith and obedience for succeeding generations. God spoke to him and told him to go to a nameless place which He would show him, and he went. He promised to make him great, a source of blessing and to make him the ancestor of a great nation. Abraham believed and acted. He packed up and left everything. The Word of God puts it this way:

> So Abram went, as the Lord had told him; and Lot went with him (Genesis 12.4)

We are left in no doubt as to the reason for his departure. Many of our reasons are mixed. Something happens, someone quarrels with someone, or they misbehave and suddenly they hear a 'thus sayeth the Lord, you have dwelt in this place long enough'. Here, Abraham left, 'as the Lord had told him'. The word of the Lord to us is made effective by our obedience to its demands. Abraham's obedience is a constant in the story of his life.

Accepting the promise

Granted, what God promised Abraham was huge, but what he had to do in response was remarkable. He went from place to place living in tents with a huge household of several hundred people plus livestock. After Lot left him, God spoke to him and reassured him of the promised inheritance, as Lot had chosen the best part of the land. Then He told him something interesting. Abraham was to walk the length and breadth of the land promised to him and he did.

A lot can happen inside you as you walk through your inheritance while it is still in the hands of other people. A few years ago, we walked the length and breadth of our city. First, we walked around the city, following the ring road. Then, we walked through the neighbourhoods, quarter by quarter, four each month, fasting and praying. One of my leaders had to confess to unbelief as we walked through one of the richest neighbourhoods in the city, she was stunned at the things I was praying and confessing. She would never have dared believe God for such things in such places.

Some dropped off from time to time then got back on board. Some walked and got excited at all the people who would be coming into the kingdom. We started again a few months before the time of finalising this book. The atmosphere was more muted, less exhilarating, but more determined and purposeful. We had matured, we had not obtained the fullness of the promise, but our faith was more robust. Whatever Abraham felt, he kept going, in obedience to divine instructions. The condition for obtaining his inheritance was obedience to God.

> The whole land of Canaan, where you now reside as a foreigner, I will give as an everlasting possession to you and your descendants after you; and I will be their God (Genesis 17:8).

He must commit to obey as must his descendants from generation to generation. And he would signal this obedience by an act of circumcision that would set him and his descendants apart for God. Abraham complied. Several hundred, including the young Ishmael, subjected themselves to a painful circumcision. To a generation like ours accustomed to having its own way, it is almost surreal. In Genesis 18:19 God says concerning Abraham that He chose him to prescribe to his descendants and his entire household to do the will of the Lord by doing what is right and just and:... so that the Lord will bring about for Abraham what he has promised him (Genesis 18.19). We will see how this plays out in the latter part of this chapter.

A TALE OF TWO SONS

One well known Christian apologist tells of speaking to a group of leading Palestinians about peace. He told the story of Abraham taking his son up to sacrifice and how

God intervened to stop him. Cleverly he said, 'never mind which son', as they believed Ishmael was the promised child. He related that to the crucifixion of Jesus the Son of God on the same mountain. He had his audience, and he made his point, a good one.

However, the Genesis account tells us that Abraham had to let Ishmael go when Sarah objected to his presence. She saw the potential for trouble over the inheritance. Abraham was deeply pained but God sided with Sarah and told him to let the boy go promising that He would bless the boy and watch over him. Think of the turmoil Abraham went through.

For thirteen years he had loved this boy. He had revelled in finally becoming a father. He had dreamed about the boy's future and their lives together. He had taught him and shared his wisdom with him. And now, he had to let him go. When we consider the circumstances in which our favourite biblical characters lived, we learn to appreciate the depth of their response to God. We also learn to obey. We understand that pain, emotion, regret cannot and must not stand in the way of complying with divine instruction. These things were written for our example. With a heavy heart, Abraham complied.

By faith, Abraham obeyed (Heb. 11:9).

A friend of God is a man of faith. He obeys by faith, knowing that God works out all things for his good. Abraham again exhibited an obedience motivated by faith many years after the incident with Ishmael. God instructed him to sacrifice Isaac, his only son. Is someone getting the picture here? But this time, it did not tell us he was deeply pained. We are told in the New Testament that he judged God able to raise him from the dead. And so on receiving the instruction, he was prompt. Note the promptitude of obedience.

The very next morning he set out. For obedience to be effective, it must be prompt. And for three days, this old father walked with his son knowing that he would soon give him up, but he obeyed. God stepped in and stopped him and testified of his obedience. A person who will have a great destiny in God must be a person of uncommon obedience, a person that God can count on.

Many years ago, a guest minister in Kensington Temple London told the story of his son. The boy was born premature and appeared to be dying. The minister had been booked for a crusade in an African country. He took his son in his arms and kissed him, thinking, this is my son, he looks like a rat. He told the baby that if on his return, he was gone, he would see him in heaven. He went off to preach and in the service, one day, God spoke to him and told him that there was a man there whose son died that morning and He wanted to bring him back to life. The man came forward, the minister prayed and God moved. And the preacher's own son was dying in a hospital in America. However, by the time he returned home, God had touched his son, the child survived and was eighteen years old when the minister told the story.

The Obedience of Noah

The testimony of ancient saints is compelling. Concerning Noah, Genesis 6 tells us that God told Noah what He was going to do. Then He told him to build an ark and told him how to build it, and how to fill it. Noah received detailed instructions on every aspect of the work. God's plans were surprising, to say the least, they were unprecedented and unimaginable, yet Noah agreed, believed and obeyed. And of Noah it is said:

> Noah did everything just as God commanded him (Genesis 6:22).

God's plans on the earth hinged on this man's obedience, and he did not fail. Only one man's family was saved from the flood. Had Noah disobeyed and not built the ark, the entire world would have been wiped out. God's plans on earth are always tied to the obedience of a human being. Obedience is not just about the convenience of a thing for you, it is about the fulfilment of divine purpose. No wonder Jesus said 'you are my friends if you do what I command'. And who better to show us the connection between obedience to God and maintaining a rich relationship with God than Jesus Himself.

The obedience of Jesus

Perhaps the most striking dimension of the life of the Master on earth was His oneness with the Father. We can easily attribute it exclusively to His divine nature and His prayer life. Yet, Jesus Himself introduced another dimension to this relationship, the dimension of obedience. Keeping His Father's commands is key to His love relationship with the Father and to our love relationship with Him.

As the Father has loved me, so have I loved you. Now remain in my love. If you keep my commands, you will remain in my love, just as I have kept my Father's commands and remain in his love. I have told you this so that my joy may be in you and that your joy may be complete (Genesis 15.9-11).

What does it mean to remain in His love? Does it mean that God would cease to love Jesus if He did not keep His commandments? Does it mean that Jesus would cease to love us were we to disobey? I believe not. Rather, it means we will not be intimate enough with Him to enjoy that love in its fullness. It means that there will be a distance that will hinder us from enjoying His pleasure. This is vital as many confuse the love of God for us and His pleasure in us. Disobedience handicaps communion.

According to Jesus, the way to remain vitally connected to God, to maintain a vibrant love relationship with Him is to be careful to do what He says to do. This is what Jesus Himself did, and that is how, as a human being, He maintained His intimacy with the Father. Obedience is key to the harmony that fosters intimacy. Elsewhere He expressed His obedience as total reliance on God in everything He said and did. He said only what He heard the Father say and did only what He saw the Father do. He turns around and tells us the same. We remain in His love by saying what He says and doing what He does.

I believe these statements of Jesus must settle the matter for us. Without obedience, there can be no deep relationship with God and no enjoyment of His many benefits. It has always been so. Obedience is a prerequisite to divine friendship.

Virtues of Obedience

Obedience - Demonstration of love for God

We have seen the example of Abraham and the example and testimony of Jesus. When the Law was given, in the same breath, the children of Israel are told both to love God and to obey Him.

> Love the Lord your God and keep his requirements, his decrees, his laws, and his commands always (Deut. 11.1).

There is no disconnection. The two go hand in hand. When we love God, when we want to be His friends, we obey Him. Jesus teaches us that love for Him is demonstrated by obedience.

> Whoever has my commands and keeps them is the one who loves me (John 14:21).

We are to love not only with words but also with deeds. Our obedience is the proof of our love for God and interest in His delight and in His kingdom. It is by the obedience of Christ that we receive redemption. God loved us and did something for us.

Obedience - a doorway to intimacy

God offers His friendship and blessing to those who obey Him. God had manifested Himself to Abraham at different times in his life. Then when Abraham was 99 years old, God gave him another encounter. He offered him a special relationship. In return, Abraham and his descendants were to keep the covenant. It would be an eternal covenant. He would give them the entire land where Abraham lived. They would be different from all other nations; they would have special access to God and be honoured above all others. But they must obey and abide by the clauses of the covenant.

> Now if you obey me fully and keep my covenant, then out of all nations you will be my treasured possession. Although the whole earth is mine (Exodus 19:5 5).

To the Christian believer, He offers intimacy. We have seen that our obedience is a demonstration of love for God. Jesus' words in John 14.21 further buttress the point. He affirms that those who love Him will obey Him. And as they do, they will receive the love of the Father and revelation of the Son. They will enjoy closeness and intimacy with God, God will make His home with them. What greater encouragement to obey can one need! Conversely, the one who does not love does not obey.

> "... The one who loves me will be loved by my Father, and I too will love them and show myself to them." Then Judas (not Judas Iscariot) said, "But, Lord, why do you intend to show yourself to us and not to the world?" Jesus replied, "Anyone who loves me will obey my teaching. My Father will love them, and we will come to them and make our home with them. Anyone who does not love me will not obey my teaching. These words you hear are not

my own; they belong to the Father who sent me." (John 14:21-24).

So the worst consequence of disobedience is not punishment, sickness or those other things that people fear. Rather, it is a loss of intimacy with and revelation of God.

OBEDIENCE - TRIGGER OF FAITHFULNESS

Obedience triggers the manifestation of divine faithfulness. God's initial promises to Abraham were unsolicited and remained unmerited, however, his conduct and obedience led to a confirmation of the promises. I think we underestimate the power of obedience, we live oblivious to God's reaction to those who do what He says. When Abraham was about to offer up his son, the voice of the Lord spoke from heaven. According to Gen 22:16-18, God swore by Himself and told Abraham that because of this singular act of obedience, He would

- surely bless him,
- make his descendants as numerous as the stars in the sky and as the sand on the seashore,
- cause his descendants to take possession of the cities of their enemies,
- cause that through his offspring all nations on earth will be blessed, and He concluded by reiterating 'because you have obeyed me.'

Notice the emphasis here is different from the other times. The promise is glorious indeed and highly detailed, but what captivates me is the reason God gives for this extraordinary set of promises. He said it was because of what Abraham had done, because of his obedience. You can feel the depth of divine emotion here. God is moved by this man's commitment to Him despite the loss to his own self. God's plan is underway. The man has done the seemingly impossible. Abraham has proven his loyalty and obedience, so the process of redemption can shift to another level. This man will do. It is as if God is saying to us, if you can take what is precious to you and give it to me, if you are willing to do something that costs you in order to be obedient to me, I will pay you back in a measure that surpasses your imagination.

> Question - Is there anything you are doing that is touching the heart of God?

The faithfulness of God extended to Abraham's descendants and the attendant benefits were also contingent on their obedience. God had told them they would be precious to Him. Now He specifies what He expects from them so that this special relationship will be maintained. His commitment is to do them good. To Abraham, He said, 'because you have obeyed', to Abraham's descendants He said in Deuteronomy 28 that their full obedience would open the door to great blessing; and proceeded to list an astounding succession of blessings. Read through the passage, it is most edifying. He promised among other things that:
- they would have primacy among all nations,
- they would be blessed in every place and geographical location,
- they would be blessed in their children

- their produce and livestock would be blessed,
- their food would be blessed,
- their every action and movement, their every endeavour would be blessed,
- they would have victory over their enemies,
- they would be blessed in their finances,
- they would always be above, always be the first and not the last.

This divine response to their obedience is enough to command our attention and emphasise the value of obedience to God. It indeed makes us a partaker of the faithfulness of God. The New Testament believer also enjoys the faithfulness of God as a consequence of obedience. Obedience brings answered prayer. The apostle John writes that when we keep the commandments of the Lord, when we do things that please Him, we receive answers to prayer.

> Dear friends, if our hearts do not condemn us, we have confidence before God and receive from him anything we ask because we keep his commands and do what pleases him. And this is his command: to believe in the name of his Son, Jesus Christ, and to love one another as he commanded us (1 John 3:21-23).

We have to believe in the name of the Son and we are to love one another as Jesus had commanded us. This is a condition for answered prayer. It is possible for a believer to do things that do not please God. Contrary to some popular teaching, God is not pleased with us irrespective of what we do. He loves us; that is a different matter entirely. That is why the Bible says that we are to find out what pleases the Lord.

The Danger of Disobedience

Disobedience kills. We know that throughout Israel's chequered history their obedience to God was inconstant. And even as obedience bears great fruit, disobedience comes at a cost. Despite the ringing promises of God to Abraham, an entire generation of his descendants did not see the Promised Land but died in the wilderness because of their disobedience. The people had to stay there until that generation died out. These were meant to be God's special people, but despite that, their end was less than glorious. We cannot take the grace of God for granted. The Israelites wandered in the wilderness for forty years until all the fighting men who had left Egypt had died, the reason?... since they had not obeyed the Lord (Joshua 5:6).

Do you see how they forfeited their blessing even though God had given His word, made a solemn promise, spoken from heaven to Abraham and sworn to give the land to his descendants? It is very sobering indeed. There is much to be learnt from this, unfortunately, the people did not learn their lesson; as we often do not.

And that is why in the book of judges, there is an encounter with the angel of the Lord where God reminded the people about His faithfulness in bringing them out of Egypt and into the Promised Land as He had sworn to do. He reminded them about His promise to not break His covenant with them, and they, in turn, were not to make any covenant with the inhabitants of the land. However, they did not obey.

... Yet you have disobeyed me. Why have you done this? (Judges 2.2).

Unfortunately, this disobedience would deprive them of total victory in the land and they would have to live alongside the ones they should have driven out. They forfeited the fullness of the manifestation of the faithfulness of God. Do you see that disobedience is a robber? It robs believers of the fullness of victory and divine friendship in their lives.

One couple did not live to tell the tale after they sinned. They sold a piece of land and brought the money to the apostle Peter for the use of the church, a worthwhile deed; save for the fact that they lied about the amount involved. They pretended that was all there was when they had set aside a portion for themselves. Their lie was exposed by the Holy Spirit and the husband fell dead. The wife came in later unaware of what happened to her husband and told the same story. She also fell dead. These were Christians, God's covenant people, and yet disobedience not only separated them from intimacy with God but led to their death. Disobedience kills.

Let us pursue intimacy with God. Some are seeking to persuade themselves and others that disobedience does not count because we are in the New Covenant, under grace. Not so. And indeed were it to be without consequence, surely a true friend of God will not even want to be at odds with the Master? God said about Abraham, he is my friend. In other words, he is with me, hears me, accepts what I say, does what I say, and I can count on him. Can God count on you? Can He count on your obedience?

It is only logical that compliance with the Master's desires and will be a prerequisite for intimacy. It is babyhood to still seek reassurance that the Master will still love you even if you disobey. We are looking here at one who is so bound to his Master that he in no way seeks allowance for disobedience, rather is desperate to be of one mind and heart with God. He is seeking the grace, the means to fully obey and comply. Seeking to be happy in disobedience is a sure sign of an uncircumcised heart and a cold love. We must beg to be made miserable were we to ever step out of God's order, for fear we would be swept away by the love of iniquity.

Which parent is happy with a child who persists in disobedience and in rebellious behaviour? Even we who are human, thus imperfect, are shocked at ungrateful behaviour. What then can be said of a man who has received the precious blood of Christ and seeks only to continue to follow his own inclinations? Can such a person be close to God? No. Jesus died not only to forgive us our sins but also to purify us and recruit us into God's company of doers of good.

Why do people disobey God?

A quick non-exhaustive list might help us avoid the pitfalls of disobedience so we do not jeopardise our intimacy with the Father.

I. Pride, arrogance, I know better

Simply put, many do not have the humility to recognise that God's way is better than theirs. They are too proud to accept, unlike Abraham in the case of Ishmael, that they should do things God's way, not theirs. They are convinced they can get to their destination following their own compass, not God's.

Even if you have started down a path before understanding you have missed it, make a u-turn and do what God wants. You may lose face with men, but you will get approval from God.

II. Weakness, fear of the consequences of obedience

Sometimes disobedience is caused by weakness of character. We must pray for the strength to tackle any challenges that come while we are doing the will of God. Some fear the potential adverse consequences on themselves of obeying God. Think of King Saul in the matter of the Amalekites. God spoke clearly to Samuel and told him that Saul had stopped following His instructions.

Interestingly, when Saul saw Samuel, the first thing he told him was that he had carried out the Lord's instructions. When Samuel accused him of not obeying the Lord, he insisted that he had obeyed the Lord and that the animals present (which he ought to have destroyed according to the instructions of the Lord through Samuel) were only taken so they could offer them as sacrifices to the Lord. This is what Samuel responds.

> Does the LORD take pleasure in burnt offerings and sacrifices as much as in obeying the LORD? Look: to obey is better than sacrifice, to pay attention is better than the fat of rams. For rebellion is like the sin of divination, and defiance is like wickedness and idolatry. Because you have rejected the word of the LORD, He has rejected you as king (1 Samuel 15:22-24).

Finally, Saul admitted to having transgressed both the commands of the Lord and Samuel's words. But listen to the reason he gave, he said that he was afraid of the people and he obeyed them. He was afraid of what the people would do if he obeyed God.

III. Foolishness, ignorance of the consequences of disobedience

Sometimes one can be too foolish to imagine the potential consequences of disobeying God. That was the case for Saul certainly. He feared the people but did not fear God. He did not think God would do anything to him for being disobedient. After all God had chosen him out of all the men in Israel. And many today are following in his footsteps. Many Christian leaders have fallen into this trap. They foolishly think themselves above the laws by which every believer must abide. So long as the anointing is still flowing, the gift is still in operation, they think their disobedience is irrelevant.

IV. Carnality, love of sin

Believe it or not, sin can be very enjoyable and some because of the temporal pleasures of sin will choose to not obey God. Many will glibly justify everything, carelessness in speaking and conduct, immorality, the list is endless. We cannot distort love to mean agreement with wrong, nor should we frown upon rebuke. Otherwise, we approve of what God hates and wallow in what He despises. How then can we be His friends?

V. Demonic influence

When the Bible says to give no room to the devil, it is precisely because he constantly seeks to exercise influence over the children of God. When the devil and his minions oppress a believer, his appetite for the things of God will be greatly diminished. This is one of the areas where Christians are shockingly insensitive. I see people neglect vital areas of their spiritual lives and refuse to take responsibility to kick the devil off their turf. The outcome is continuous disobedience.

VI. Wrong counsellors

Wrong counsel can amputate a destiny. I have seen many believers on fire for God gradually lose their zeal and slide into coldness, criticism and compromise. And all because they began to follow and listen to the wrong persons in the church. They stopped doing the things that caused their hearts to burn for God. Over the years many have tried to get me to take it easy and not be so intense about God.

They would even mock and try to prove to you that they are just as blessed if not more than you despite all your intensity. But it is not about being blessed, it is about pleasing God. May you be deaf to foolish counsel. I once wrote a lengthy article on the unfortunate fate of a son and a grandson of David. Both men suffered from taking counsel from the wrong quarters. Even though God was against them both, it was through the agency of wrong counsel that their discomfiting occurred. I wrote in the article that 'when someone seeks to direct your life with their words, influence your thinking with their opinions, ask God if this person is sent of Him to you, of themselves to you or of the devil to you.'

Conclusion

Whatever the reasons people give for disobedience, let us never forget that we have an example of obedience in Abraham. And it ended well for him. God Himself testifies to that through the prophet Isaiah.

> Listen to me, you who pursue righteousness and who seek the Lord: Look to the rock from which you were cut and to the quarry from which you were hewn; look to Abraham, your father, and to Sarah, who gave you birth. When I called him he was only one man, and I blessed him and made him many (Isaiah 51:1-2).

2.5

COMMUNE WITH HIM

We proclaim to you what we have seen and heard, so that you also may have fellowship with us. And our fellowship is with the Father and with his Son, Jesus Christ (1 John 1:3).

IMAGINE SHARING A FLAT WITH A PERSON and hardly ever speaking to them. You may even live in the same room but you have next to no interaction with them. You never stop to talk, eat, fellowship together. You may say a quick good morning and off you go.

Mealtimes are never shared. And when you do speak, it is to complain and grumble about some problem you think they have caused you, some difficulty you want them to resolve. And when it is resolved you mumble a thank you, tell them how sweet they are for five minutes and by the next day you are again entrenched behind your wall of silence and busyness. Before long the friendship will be soured and one of you will be house hunting fast.

Some people are like that with God. They barely speak to Him, save for a quick 'Praise the Lord' in the morning and off they go. They have oh, such busy lives and no time to squeeze out for prayer and Bible study. But when things go awry, they complain vociferously to God. They grudgingly give a quick thank you and an 'I love you Lord' when blessings come but immediately retreat into their busyness only to re-emerge for conversation at the next challenge. That is not the way of friendship and it will do nothing to strengthen our relationship with God.

Let's break this down. We were God's enemies, now we are His friends. Friends relate, friends commune and friends communicate. In other words, friends fellowship. Fellowship involves sharing, communicating, giving of oneself, of one's time; it is enjoying one another, it is spending time loving one another. That is what God wants from His friends. God desires us to be intimate, to be close to Him; not just 'good' Christians. Those who have become, as the apostle Peter puts it, 'partakers of the divine nature' are empowered to live in closeness with the possessor of the divine nature.

Testimonies of communion with God

From the word go, God's desire to commune with His friends was obvious in His relationship with the first man and woman. They had fellowship with God. Unfortunately, they lost their first estate but in Christ, communion and intimacy are once again offered to mankind. What shall we say about Abraham?

The case of Abraham

> Abram travelled through the land as far as the site of the great tree of Moreh at Shechem. At that time the Canaanites were in the land. The Lord appeared to Abram and said, 'To your offspring, I will give this land.' So he built an altar there to the Lord, who had appeared to him (Genesis 12:6).

God had appeared to Abraham before he went to Canaan and had spoken to him. So Abraham knew the voice of God, was able to recognise the presence of God and receive instructions from Him. Fellowship for him was different from fellowship in the Spirit for us, but it is clear that he was a man who sought the presence of God. God encountered him in dreams, visions and diverse revelations. He would frequently set up altars to worship the Lord.

And on one occasion, in Genesis 18, we see another dimension of fellowship between God and Abraham. God appeared to him in human form. He came with two angels and Abraham hosted Him. He sat and talked to Abraham about the impending birth of Isaac. And when

He was leaving, He spoke to him about the destruction of the cities of the plain. Abraham, on the basis of this fellowship, pleaded for Sodom and Gomorrah to be spared. This is God making classified information available to His friend Abraham in the place of fellowship. Jesus said I call you friends because what I have learnt from my Father I have shown to you (John 15.15).

This is a picture of the intimacy and nearness in which we are to live with God—that He be able to speak to us as one speaking to a friend (Exodus 33:11). By virtue of the new birth, access has been given us into that dimension of closeness and togetherness. Abraham fellowshipped with God as a man around a meal. God is not an alien deity whom we implore from afar. No, we have been brought near, and we are enjoined to ourselves draw near. The Father and the Son have come to dwell in us.

> Jesus replied, 'Anyone who loves me will obey my teaching. My Father will love them, and we will come to them and make our home with them,' (John 14:23).

The case of Enoch

Bear with me, but I imagine the story may have gone like this. Let's say, perhaps Enoch went for a walk with a friend and in the course of the conversation, the friend looked away to point at something in the distance. He looked back again and his companion was gone. He searched high and low, troubled that some bad men may have laid their hands on him. But how could that have happened, he had grunted in response to him barely thirty seconds before? He went back to the town, told everyone what had happened, and they launched a search for the missing man. The men returned at sunset still puzzled.

The next morning Enoch's son Methuselah awakens from a shocking dream in which the Most High God, the God of His father revealed to him that He had taken away the missing man. Methuselah relays this information to the community and the entire community bows in worship. There are so many ways it could have happened, the Bible does not relate the exact circumstances. All we are told is that Enoch walked with God and he was no more because God took him (Genesis 5:24).

You can hardly find a shorter description of a man of God in the Bible than that given of Enoch. In just a few words, the entire life of a man is explained. He was married, bore children, walked with God and God took him, and that is all that mattered. One is reminded of the song lyrics that say 'Only what's done for Christ will last'. Why preoccupy oneself with so much that has no lasting value? These things pass and the only thing that matters is what the Bible says about Enoch. It is fleshed out slightly, only very slightly in Hebrews 11.

> By faith, Enoch was taken from this life so that he did not experience death: "He could not be found because God had taken him away." For before he was taken, he was commended as one who pleased God (Hebrews 11:5).

This is the essential quality of any man; faith in God, fellowship with God, eternity with God. Enoch had all three. He trusted Him, lived in communion with Him and ended up with Him. What will be on your epitaph? Something is going to be said about you when you die. Choose it now. I have decided that on my tombstone, I want them to write that I was a friend of God. That is my preferred summary of my life. She was a friend of God, she walked with God.

The case of Noah

In Genesis 6:9, there is a stirring testimony to the life of one man.

> This is the account of Noah and his family. Noah was a righteous man, blameless among the people of his time, and he walked faithfully with God (Genesis 6:9).

Here is another one who walked with God. The interesting thing about Noah was that he was alone. You will often find yourself alone when you are determined to follow God. Wisdom does not follow the crowd. But he was unwavering in his commitment to the Lord. While others were feasting and revelling, He was communing with God. Some may have mocked his piety and told him to loosen up, yet, he steadfastly walked with God.

We must walk with God in the face of incomprehension, mockery, derision, and antagonism. The need of the hour is for Christians who, like Abraham have thrown their lot in with God and will stand against the secularisation of the faith oblivious to derision and antagonism. That is what it takes to be a true friend of God rather than a fair-weather friend.

THE CASE OF MOSES

True friends always want more intimacy. Such was Moses who spoke 'face to face' with God. The man had experienced diverse encounters with God since the burning bush encounter. He had been up the mountain of the Lord, communed deeply with God and yet craved more of God. Our hearts must crave more as we fellowship.

Many years ago, God graciously began to deal with my heart and draw me more deeply into fellowship with Him. I would wait on the Lord and cry out to know Him and the more I saw, the more I wanted. Exodus 33 became a life Scripture. How does a man speak face to face with God? Should that even be allowed? If it was permitted under the Old Covenant, are you not entitled to covet it under the New? Jesus may not come and sit in your living room to chat with you visibly, but He will more than possess your heart and consume you with His Person.

Then Moses said, 'Now show me your glory' (Exodus 33:18).

And when, despite the previous encounters, Moses craved more of God's revelation, God granted his request.

THE TESTIMONY OF JESUS

Our Lord lived in symbiosis with the Father and the Holy Spirit. In John 14:11, He is quoted as saying:

I am in the Father and the Father is in me.

He drew alone often to be in communion with the Father. He went to lonely places, fled the crowds, and stayed up all night. Jesus showed us how a human being could live in fellowship with God. He lived such that he knew what God was saying and doing and He did and said the same. That is huge! What God wants is a people who think like Him, see as He sees and acts as He acts. Our Lord was a perfect embodiment of that.

Living like the Master

In the new birth, we who were far have been brought near. The nearness to God must settle in our spirits. We were outsiders, now we are family members. We can come boldly to the throne. We can receive the revelation that is the privilege of those He calls friends. We can enjoy the closeness to God that Jesus enjoyed here. We have been saved from hell, saved from sin and saved to intimacy.

Indeed 1 Corinthians 1.9 testifies that 'God is faithful, who has called you into fellowship with his Son, Jesus Christ our Lord'. So we have a calling, to live in fellowship with Jesus. Our destiny is intense communication with God.

> What agreement is there between the temple of God and idols? For we are the temple of the living God. As God has said: 'I will live with them and walk among them, and I will be their God, and they will be my people.' (2 Corinthians 6:16).

Where there is incompatibility of nature, there must be a break in fellowship. However, God has made us sharers in His nature and thus granted potential for sweet communion.

> "Our communion, then, with God consists in His communication of Himself unto us, with our return unto Him of that which He requires and accepts, flowing from that union which in Jesus Christ we have with Him[4]"
> John Owen

How then do we develop our communion with God?

DEVELOPING CLOSENESS WITH GOD

The avowed intent behind the revelations shared in the first letter of John is to bring the recipients to a place of fellowship/communion. And the communion we all have and are meant to have is with the Father and the Son. We know that includes the Holy Spirit and Scripture bears it out. The goal is a community of love, sharing, loving and enjoying God together. This fellowship with one another and with God issues in great joy.

> We proclaim to you what we have seen and heard, so that you also may have fellowship with us. And our fellowship is with the Father and with his Son, Jesus Christ. We write this to make our joy complete (1 John 1:3-4).

Every child of God has been positioned in relationship with God in the new birth, but the experience of that relationship differs from person to person. How do we

---

[4] Owen, J. (1808). Of Communion with God the father, son & holy ghost (each person distinctly) in love, grace, & consolation: Or, The saints fellowship with the father, son and holy ghost, unfolded. London: W. Nicholson.

develop the deep closeness with God that characterises a friend of God? What are the different facets of this fellowship? We will examine five essential points.

1. Scriptural revelation
2. Walking in the light
3. A passion for His presence
4. Prayer and worship
5. Deference

Scriptural revelation

Everyone who comes to God must know that He exists, and that He is a rewarder of those who seek Him, according to Hebrews 11. Two things come to play here. First, we must acknowledge the reality of His Person, and secondly, we must recognise His true nature. In other words, we must know God as He truly is. That, in essence, is the first principle of true intimate communion for divine friendship. Come to God as He is, not as you will like Him to be. To develop true fellowship, you must set aside your notions of God or your list of what you would like God to be and do. Rather, delve into His Word to flesh out and understand His character so as to have an accurate picture of Him.

We can only be close to God as we see His true Self not the God of our imagination. A person may fashion 'God' after their desires and based on their needs. Such a person will have an emotional and non-spiritual relationship with God. This causes confusion in their souls, and they are wont to attribute to God thoughts, ideas, etc. that emanate from their own deep-seated desires. This, unfortunately, can sometimes go very far. Endeavour to seek a true picture of God in His Word. How do the Scriptures portray Him? What does He say of Himself?

True Scriptural revelation of God causes our hearts to be captivated by Him and nurtures our affection for the Master. There is a connection between seeing Him in His Word and loving Him profoundly. Once again, we must have an accurate picture of God. As that picture becomes more and more distinct in our minds, our esteem and admiration grow, and our fellowship with Him is thereby enriched. Prayer ceases to be a chore, it becomes a privilege and an honour. With some people, the more you know them, the less enthusiastic about them you become. The reverse is true of God. Communion grows as Scriptural revelation grows.

I was convinced otherwise as a non-believer and it plagued me when I became a Christian. There was an irrational fear that lurking somewhere in the pages of Scripture, in particular, the Old Testament were things that I could not agree with. So I thought that if I were to delve into the Bible, I was bound to find something that would destroy my faith.

Walk in the Light

To live in intimacy with God as a true friend, we must walk in the light. Perhaps the most important Scriptural revelation of God is that He is holy. The apostle John testifies as such:

> This is the message we have heard from him and declare to you: God is light; in him, there is no

darkness at all. If we claim to have fellowship with him and yet walk in the darkness, we lie and do not live out the truth. But if we walk in the light, as he is in the light, we have fellowship with one another, and the blood of Jesus, his Son, purifies us from all sin... (1 John 1:5-7).

Light means purity, truth, holiness. God is a Being of perfect virtue and truth. No darkness, that is, evil, sin, impurity can be found in Him. So anyone who will be His friend and be always in fellowship with Him must of necessity adapt himself to God. Reread verse 6 of this passage. We cannot claim to have fellowship with him if we are walking in darkness, we would be lying and not living out the truth.

Does this, as some commentators believe, refer to non-believers who may want to claim to be Christians? I think not. Indeed, the Word of God says that believers are in the light and are children of the light, yet it also warns us against adopting the works of darkness, which means that children of the Light can choose to walk in darkness. But those who want fellowship with God must choose to walk in the light. True friends of God walk in the light and not in darkness.

What is walking in darkness? Ephesians chapter five sheds great light on the concept of light and darkness as it pertains to the believer. We are quoting a fairly long portion of the chapter because it holds powerful nuggets of truth. Read through slowly, underline the passages and let it sink in.

> Follow God's example, therefore, as dearly loved children and live a life of love, just as Christ loved us and gave himself up for us as a fragrant offering and sacrifice to God. But among you, there must not be even a hint of sexual immorality, or of any kind of impurity, or of greed, because these are improper for God's holy people. Nor should there be obscenity, foolish talk or coarse joking, which are out of place, but rather thanksgiving. For of this you can be sure: no immoral, impure or greedy person – such a person is an idolater – has any inheritance in the kingdom of Christ and of God. Let no one deceive you with empty words, for because of such things God's wrath comes on those who are disobedient. Therefore do not be partners with them. For you were once darkness, but now you are light in the Lord. Live as children of light (for the fruit of the light consists in all goodness, righteousness, and truth) and find out what pleases the Lord. Have nothing to do with the fruitless deeds of darkness, but rather expose them. It is shameful even to mention what the disobedient do in secret. But everything exposed by the light becomes visible – and everything that is illuminated becomes a light. This is why it is said: 'Wake up, sleeper, rise from the dead, and Christ will shine on you.' (Ephesians 5:1-14)

From verses 3 to 8 the apostle is talking about the lifestyle of those who walk in darkness. He says 'do not do these things; it is the disobedient that do them, and God is angry with them for it. You used to be in darkness but now you are in the light, so live differently now,'. What does walking in darkness look like?

- It is to walk in sin,
- It is to redefine sin,
- It is to deny that we have any sin,
- It is to justify sin,
- It is to fail to repent of sin.

The believer must flee these things because a person walking in darkness cannot have true fellowship with the Father.

What is walking in the light? Ephesians 5:1, 9-10 give us some clarity on the matter:

- It is being an imitator of God.
- It is following the example of Jesus.
- It is avoiding known sin.
- It is walking in goodness, righteousness, and truth.
- It is doing what pleases the Lord.

We are then enjoined to be 'very careful' how we live, to be 'wise', to 'not be foolish'. It will behove us to take this to heart. Unfortunately, many believers do the opposite. They are not at all careful how they live, they do not know what God's will is, so they get into a lot of trouble and are constantly complaining about not hearing God, feeling God, sensing God, not being loved of God, etc., etc. We are to ascertain what pleases the Lord, what His will is and do it.

How do we do this? By the power of the Holy Spirit working in us, showing us the things of God, changing our desires, causing us to want what God wants, and to do what God wants. It is making a deliberate choice to live 'in a manner worthy of the Lord'. So the way we live will determine how close we are to God. When we live in continual and flagrant violation of God's standards of life, we declare ourselves unreliable friends who either do not agree with His standards or do not respect them.

Do not get drunk on wine, which leads to debauchery. Instead, be filled with the Spirit, speaking to one another with psalms, hymns, and songs from the Spirit. Sing and make music from your heart to the Lord, always giving thanks to God the Father for everything, in the name of our Lord Jesus Christ (Ephesians 5:18-20).

And the jewel in the crown is that all of this leads us to a life of praise, worship, making music in our hearts to the Lord, a lifestyle of deep fellowship and enjoyment of divine friendship.

> FIND GOD IN HIS WORD - YOU MAY HAVE COME TO HIM INITIALLY FOR YOUR NEEDS, BUT GO BEYOND YOUR NEEDS OR YOU WILL NEVER BE A TRUE FRIEND OF GOD.

PASSION FOR HIS PERSON AND PRESENCE

Many years ago, it hit me that if God is God, and is all that the Bible says that He is, then fellowshipping with Him should be a delight and not a chore. So I began to pray and ask for that to become my experience. God answered. Dutiful obedience is good but a heart aflame for God is God's ideal. We do not always think of God in that light but, we were made to desire God. Without deep-seated desire, we are quickly distracted, prayer becomes monotonous, worship becomes an imposition, our flesh craves escape into worldly pursuits, and our mind wanders. Things that should delight us begin to weigh on us. The psalmist cries out in Psalm 63, verse 10:

> God, you are my God; earnestly I seek you; my soul thirsts for you; my flesh faints for you, as in a dry and weary land where there is no water.

If we do not have this holy desire, we can ask for it. And even if we have it we should ask for more. We can never be excessive in holy desire. So pray that your very being will crave the Person and presence of God. Cry out for holy desire. We cannot make ourselves desire God, love His company, or enjoy prayer; but if we ask, He will do it in and for us. What manner of friend flees the presence of the other?

Indifference towards God is a grave malady of the church of the 21st century. We love our services, our songs, our slogans and all the paraphernalia of worship, but we are not caught up in the One who is the Object of our worship. So pray, beloved, pray. Do not be satisfied until you begin to experience heart to heart encounters with God. That is the life of a friend of God, deep-seated, day-to-day connection in worship. Once again, hear the cry of the psalmist.

> I have seen you in the sanctuary and beheld your power and your glory. Because your love is better than life, my lips will glorify you (Psalm 63:2-3).

Acknowledge God's worth and celebrate Him

To honour is to acknowledge a person's worth in word and deed. We acknowledge God's worth in words by speaking His greatness, goodness, and love. We call it praise.

> I will praise you as long as I live, and in your name, I will lift up my hands. I will be fully satisfied as with the richest of foods; with singing lips, my mouth will praise you (Psalm 63:4-5).

Let your lips glorify Him. Singing and praising God, pouring out love and adoration to Him causes us to see Him more clearly, and it nurtures this divine friendship. Do it night and day

> On my bed I remember you; I think of you through the watches of the night. Because you are my help, I sing in the shadow of your wings. I cling to you; your right hand upholds me (Psalm 63:6-8).

He is praising, lifting up his hands, and he is fully satisfied; he is singing, meditating on God all night, clinging to God and God sustains him. This is a divine exchange; we love, we worship, God satisfies and sustains and the intimacy grows.

Pray

Prayer is a wonderful place of encounter with God. It is the place where you, as His friend, take your place as His representative on the earth to work for the furtherance of His interests. Before Jesus left the earth, He taught His disciples and us to pray. In what we call the 'Lord's prayer' He taught us priorities in prayer. First, we honour the name of the Lord, then we pray for the manifestation of His kingdom and His will on the earth. This is the heart of a friend of God—that the purposes, ways of God become manifest reality.

As a friend of God, you will honour the Lord by honouring His name and by devoting time to pray for His kingdom, His church, His people and for the manifestation of His will on the earth. In so doing, you show that you care. Then, you will pray for your own needs which He will be glad to meet. If we only pray for the things we want and need for our lives, we demonstrate an indifference towards the desires of God that is not fitting for friends of God.

Let prayer be a regular affair. Abraham set up altars to the Lord at specific times and places. An altar is a place of encounter. Everyone must have a place and a time of encounter. The psalmist says in Psalm 119:164, "Seven times a day I praise you for your righteous laws." Daniel, we are told, prayed by the window three times a day. Jesus rose early to pray in isolated places. He would on occasion pray all night. Everyone needs a place where they are physically alone with God.

Set aside a place of communion with God every day. If it is left to chance, it will soon peter away. Every child of God must live by divine principle, not by emotions. There must be steadiness and stability in our time of prayer and fellowship. Whatever is not planned will not be done. Think carefully, plan and execute. We do not function purely by instinct. Oh, I felt a touch, and I prayed for five hours and when I do not feel a touch, I do not pray.

An altar is a place of sacrifice. Whatever you have to give up spending time with God, do it. An altar is a place of divine promise. As you fellowship with the Lord, you will step into a revelation of the great and precious promises that are your inheritance in Christ, not least of which is His promise to make His home in you.

Pray without ceasing. Walk the streets talking to God. Listen to Him as you drive or commute to work. Engage in continuous interaction with Him. Your days will be rich and your nights pleasant.

PUT HIM ON THE THRONE, DEFER TO HIM

Whatever you do, set Him on the throne of your life. Defer to Him in everything. He will beautify your existence.

> It is an unquantifiable privilege to have the ear of God![5]

A BEAUTIFUL EXISTENCE

Friend of God, in developing your communion with God, you will experience
- A deep consciousness of God
- Stronger faith–certainty concerning the things of God
- Intimacy–knowing God's heart
- Peace, rest, fullness of joy in His presence
- Answered prayer
- Greater sensitivity to the needs of the kingdom

---

5   OGEDENGBE, B. (2016). EYE TO THE CROWN: A lifestyle for ultimate victory. Paris: Beautiful Books.

- Separation from the world
- A tender heart towards others, greater love for the brethren.

Welcome to a beautiful existence.

2.6

HONOUR HIM

'A son honours his father, and a slave his master. If I am a father, where is the honour due to me? If I am a master, where is the respect due to me?' says the Lord Almighty (Malachi 1:6).

IN THE BOOK OF MALACHI, THE VOICE of God sounds out to correct His people of major failings in their relationship with Him. The people had returned from captivity, rebuilt the temple and re-instituted the sacrifices. The only problem was, they were offering God the worst kind of animals for sacrifice in direct violation of His laws requiring that only the first and the best must be brought to Him. He reminds them of His greatness, and that since He was their Father, He deserved to be honoured. Indeed, no vital, intimate relationship can be forged without honour. True friends of God will honour Him.

There is a place in God when we go beyond the 'Lord, do you love me'? God is love and is immutable. There is a place where we turn our attention to 'Lord, do I love you enough, do I honour You'? We cease trying to get God to be good to us, and we choose to start being good to God. Does God need our goodness? No, but He values it. That is when our focus is on how am I treating God rather than how is God treating me? Am I the way I ought to be with the Lord? These people in Malachi's day were not the way they ought to be with God. Their attitude toward Him was wrong. God said they despised Him. And they were surprised, as it had perhaps never occurred to them that their attitude was one of disdain.

We also may have attitudes and ways of behaving that reflect a measure of disdain for God. The very thought sounds horrific, yet it is not one we should casually dismiss. We were not reconciled with God on the basis of our personal goodness, rather, despite our lack of it. Consequently, the onus is on us to allow God to work in us and move us towards greater goodness in life and conduct. Indeed the quality of your relationship with God and the depth of your friendship with Him will depend on the degree of change you accept in your life. As we accept the change, we cease to dishonour and begin to honour God.

The word 'Kabod' was translated into glory or honour. It means weighty. The Greek word 'timao' is rendered as honour; it speaks of valuables of great price. To honour God is to recognise His great worth, to esteem Him highly. It is to consider Him, and all that pertains to Him weighty, of extreme importance, and to treat them with the utmost respect.

We are creatures deeply affected by the visible and material realm. Say, for instance, I had to walk the twenty-something odd kilometres from Paris to Versailles. If on the way, as I was close to exhaustion, someone were to stop and offer to take me there in their car, I would gladly accept the offer. At that point, a car, for me would be a thing of great worth. Its value would be immediately apparent to me. The same goes for a person on the verge of being evicted from their home; someone showed up and paid off the bank. That person would be held in high honour.

The honour we grant to the man who watches our house at night and who we pay slightly above the minimum wage is not the same as the honour given to the mayor of the city who himself receives slightly less honour than the president of the nation. Honour is proportional to perceived greatness, usefulness and assistance rendered. God is invisible and the degree of honour we give Him is commensurate with our perception of the value of the non-material, of our need and His response to that need. It is connected to our understanding of His greatness and His infinite worth.

How did Abraham honour God?

Abraham exhibited a degree of honour for God that is worthy of emulation. He did so despite the relatively limited scope of revelation, the absence of written Scriptures, of centuries of divine revelation. Yet under the New Covenant, we are compelled to go even further than our father Abraham did.

Abraham honoured the Lord with the trust that he exhibited in His promises. The Word of God says that he did not waver concerning God's promises. This enables us to better interpret the incidents of the life of Abraham and understand his response to God. We have seen how the man persisted in wandering from place to place in a foreign land based solely on what God had said to him; there were no external signs that it would be so. And so his confidence in God was an expression of honour.

He honoured God in His unqualified obedience and in his full commitment to God's plans and purposes. He was wholly engaged with his heart and mind in following God and doing His will. His worship was both consistent and thorough. We never hear of God chiding him over the quality of his sacrifice, he did it right. God blessed him and he honoured the Lord with what he possessed. Of his own free will, he presented the tithe to Melchizedek, the priest of the Lord. And the book of Hebrews, in drawing a parallel between Melchizedek and Jesus, testifies to the significance of this one gesture. Everything about his life showed the high esteem in which he held God. Our lives must do the same.

How do we honour God?

How do we show proper respect for God? One day one of my little nephews teasingly called his father, my brother by his nickname. My brother and I jokingly commented on the fact that he would never have dared call our father by his nickname when he was his son's age. It would have been considered shocking and most disrespectful. In fact, he said, the thought would never have occurred to him. For his son, however, it was not disrespectful, as he had been raised differently. He was following the standards his father had set as appropriate behaviour. The question is what are the standards of behaviour that God has set for us? What does He consider as being the honourable way to treat Him?

Gratitude

To honour God is to show gratitude. All we have is from Him. A profoundly grateful person thinks good thoughts about God and does not cease to bless Him. The psalms ring out with calls for thanksgiving and shouts of gratitude.

> Those who sacrifice thank offerings honour me, and to the blameless, I will show my salvation (Psalm 50:23).

Gratitude is to be cultivated most assiduously. We are too often self-centred and ungrateful. Not only do we not value the price others pay to assist us, but we also do not remember long enough the good they did us. We need a continuous revelation of the cross that we may be ceaselessly overwhelmed by the greatness of the sacrifice of Christ and the depth of the love of God. We must pray for grateful hearts that never cease to marvel that such a glorious Being would consider us His children.

Cultivating a grateful attitude towards the Lord will also protect us from grumbling and complaining in times of hardship and thus dishonouring God. Some people rail against God when they are going through hard times. Whatever else is happening in the world, this one thing, the only thing that counts, is right. I belong to God. Nothing happening in the natural world can counterbalance the relationship with the Living God that I am privileged to enjoy. And I have no intention of souring that relationship by reacting negatively to outside events.

So many times people get up and testify movingly of what God has done in their lives and you rejoice with them and marvel at the bountifulness of God. In no time at all, however, they are frustrated and discouraged and sometimes acting up because of some challenge in their lives. Beloved, God is always good; we live in a fallen world replete with challenges to face and mountains to conquer. Settle in your heart that God is your benefactor not your torturer, your solution and not your problem, and never stop thanking Him.

Thank Him as you awaken, thank Him as you leave home, thank Him on your way to work, thank Him throughout the day, thank Him as you lay your head down to sleep. Thank Him for the breath He released into you, for the blood that courses through your veins, for love, for life, for peace, for hope, for every material good, for all that is right in your life. Thank Him for the cross and for eternal life. Once you get going, you will find it almost impossible to stop.

To thank Him is to honour Him. It is to say that He is the Source of all good, the Architect of all grace. To thank Him is to acknowledge that He is God and that there is no one like Him. It is to express His supremacy and omniscience and to say, in the words of Isaiah:

> Do you not know? Have you not heard? Has it not been told you from the beginning? Have you not understood since the earth was founded? He sits enthroned above the circle of the earth, and its people are like grasshoppers. He stretches out the heavens like a canopy and spreads them out like a tent to live in. He brings princes to naught and reduces the rulers of this world to nothing.... "To whom will you compare me? Or who is my equal?" says the Holy One. Lift up your eyes and look to the heavens: Who created all these? He who brings out the starry host one by one and calls forth each of them by name. Because of his great power and mighty strength, not one of them is missing (Isaiah 40:21-26).

FINANCES

Another important way of honouring God is by presenting Him with a part of the wealth He has given us. We read in the book of Proverbs:

> Honour the Lord with your wealth, with the firstfruits of all your crops; then your barns will be

filled to overflowing, and your vats will brim over with new wine (Proverbs 3:9-10).

There are some vital principles in this passage and in the following ones as to how we honour God with our possessions.

- We are supposed to give.
- We give to God first before we spend anything on ourselves. The first fruits the Israelites were instructed to bring to God were the first portion of the crops. We cannot justify not giving by saying we have nothing left.
- We give to God the best that we have. The incident of the diseased animals being offered in Malachi's time illustrates the need to give in a way worthy of the Lord.
- We give what costs us something. God gave His Son, asked for Abraham's son and then spared him. David understood this and said as much when he bought Araunah's field for sacrifice. The striking thing is that Araunah the Jebusite offered to give him the land to be used for free, in other words, minimal stress, minimal effort, minimal or rather zero expenditure. David turned down the offer. He said he could not possibly offer to the Lord his God something that cost him nothing. He would rather pay for it. What a lesson for us all.

> No, but I will surely buy it from you for a price; nor will I offer burnt offerings to the LORD my God with that which costs me nothing (2 Samuel 24:24).

- He gave massively for the building of the temple

and Solomon sacrificed unimaginable numbers of animals to the Lord at its inauguration.

We do not honour the Lord when we dig deep into our bags to fish out a coin or a rumpled bill at offering time. Give regularly, generously and in a manner that honours the Lord. We see Abraham presenting his tithe to Melchizedek who was a priest of God and he received a blessing. He did it willingly and clearly with a sense of privilege. In return, he received a blessing.

Honour His name - Respect for God's reputation

Immediately after Abraham presented his tithe to Melchizedek, something interesting occurred. The king of Sodom whose land Abraham had more or less liberated wanted to offer him all the spoil. Abraham declined. This is what transpired.

> The king of Sodom said to Abram, "Give me the people and keep the goods for yourself." But Abram said to the king of Sodom, "With raised hand I have sworn an oath to the Lord, God Most High, Creator of heaven and earth, that I will accept nothing belonging to you, not even a thread or the strap of a sandal, so that you will never be able to say, 'I made Abram rich.' I will accept nothing but what my men have eaten and the share that belongs to the men who went with me—to Aner, Eshkol, and Mamre. Let them have their share (Genesis 15:21-24).

Can you see the dynamics here? Somehow Abraham knew that the king of Sodom would boastfully say that it was thanks to him that Abraham became wealthy, and

Abraham would have none of it. He preferred to turn his back on material gain rather than to have God's glory given to another. In an age when believers are breaking all the rules to acquire wealth, where financial gain at all costs has become the mantra of many a churchgoer, we will do well to heed this example. God is our Source and it must be seen in the way we live.

Integrity in our affairs honours God. Leaning on Him in trying times honours Him. Trusting Him rather than making compromises honours Him. We cannot take gifts from people whose hands are soiled with blood, against the witness of the Spirit and think we can walk in intimacy with God. Our business and all our affairs must be conducted in a manner that gives glory to God. How else do we honour God? To honour God is to worship Him as He desires to be worshipped.

Worship

The prophet Malachi gave voice to God's displeasure of the people for bringing Him the worst offerings imaginable. The substance of their worship and their attitude in their worship violated his principles and consequently were unacceptable and insulting. We must be careful to worship God in truth, with pure hearts and clean hands and allow the Holy Spirit to direct us. Let us not lift unholy hands to Him.

Honour God by taking the appointment for worship service seriously. Be punctual, come with an eager heart and expectant spirit, and be the first to jump up excitedly to offer Him praise. Many do not seem to realise that sauntering in casually when the worship has started is gravely disrespectful of God. And they will not attempt such behaviour with human authorities. Yes, the way we behave around the things of God matters. The way we conduct His affairs matter. Watch how God rebuked the people for their behaviour:

> "When you offer blind animals for sacrifice, is that not wrong? When you sacrifice lame or diseased animals, is that not wrong? Try offering them to your governor! Would he be pleased with you? Would he accept you?" says the Lord Almighty. "Now plead with God to be gracious to us. With such offerings from your hands, will he accept you?" — says the Lord Almighty (Malachi 1:8-9).

He called their altar fires useless and categorically said He was not pleased with them and would not accept their offerings. They were giving to God what they would not have dared to give to the governor. The principle is clear. No human should receive greater honour or respect from us than what we give to God. There is need for greater reverence in our dealings with Him. We must learn what in God's eyes constitutes proper conduct.

This in no way denies the New Covenant, nor are we saying that we achieve salvation through these things. But we are to put on the new man and live in a manner worthy of the Lord. God's Word is a constant reminder that there is a way of life that is befitting for a born-again child of God. Paramount to this lifestyle is our fear of God and our intimacy with the Father.

We are reminded of the conundrum in which Eli the priest found himself. His two sons Hophni and Phineas were men of carnal appetites with a distinctly unspiritual bent. They had no respect for the Lord and dishonoured Him publicly. They made a mockery of the worship of God as they helped themselves at the Lord's altar and conducted ungodly relationships with the female worshippers. We sometimes forget that there have always been predators at the altar. These men displeased the Lord greatly because of their disdain for Him. And the word of the Lord came to Eli; he was soundly rebuked for 'scorning' the prescribed sacrifice and offering. Notice that God had Himself prescribed the manner of the worship to be offered to Him. To Eli He said:

> Why do you honour your sons more than me by fattening yourselves on the choice parts of every offering made by my people Israel?' "Therefore the Lord, the God of Israel, declares: 'I promised that members of your family would minister before me forever.' But now the Lord declares: 'Far be it from me! Those who honour me I will honour, but those who despise me will be disdained (1 Samuel 2:29-30).

We are privileged under the New Covenant to have the Holy Spirit who leads us into all truth and by whom we worship the Father in Spirit and in truth. We must guard against attitudes in worship that demonstrate disrespect for God. Friends of God are those who honour God. And as they honour Him, He will honour them.

Service - Taking the service of God seriously

We honour God by taking what pertains to Him and His kingdom seriously. A true friend of God is a servant of the kingdom of God. As friends, we share the same desires and ambitions. We care about what God cares about and want to be a part of it. Indifference to the work of the kingdom is one of the sure signs of a lack of intimacy with God. When you are truly close to God, He will communicate His desires to you, you will share His heart.

I have seen people wander from church to church talking about their deep fellowship with the Lord and the great revelations they receive from Him while exhibiting no interest in the work of God. They do not truly know Him because they do not care about Him or about His purposes.

Ask yourself, how useful am I to God? How useful am I to my local church? What contribution am I making so that the Lamb that was slain will receive the reward of His suffering? We do not love God in word only, but in deed as well. God is always giving people things to do. When He made man, He ordered them to do something, namely, subdue the earth. He called David and gave him work to do. He called Paul and gave him work to do, and to all believers, He gave the job of making disciples of all nations. Are you working for God?

I once heard a pastor say that in the early days of their church they had a lot of broken people show up. They took care of them and helped them to break through. They, understandably thought that once the people were on their feet, they would participate in the work of the kingdom and help to build the church. But they did not.

Rather, as soon as they were restored, they got busy with their own lives and the work of God continued to suffer. And this happened with wave after wave of people. Yet these believers would gleefully sing about being a friend of God.

Get busy working for God. He does not love you any more because you do, but He honours you when you honour Him. You cannot give your all to your career and little or no effort to the work of God, to building the church which is the pillar of truth, to winning souls and to making disciples, which is the grand enterprise of the Most High God.

Some people chafe at the cost; they would rather watch enemies of God on television and soak in entertainment that fights their faith. Over the years as a pastor, I have seen people either refuse to commit to serve or jump in to do something and then back out when even minimal effort is required of them. They grumble, complain, gossip and sink into the cesspit of the flesh. Someone lied to them that serving God was supposed to be easy and should not cost anything.

The people building the wall in the time of Nehemiah knew better. They worked under very trying conditions and were subjected to attacks, persecution, backbiting, and fatigue. When they grew weary, they began to lose heart, but Nehemiah encouraged them. They accepted that fatigue did not mean the work should not go on. They were refreshed, and they continued. They honoured the Lord and His work prospered in their hands. In 52 days, the wall was built.

Faith in God—Distrust is Dishonour

Abraham was commended for his faith because he made the decision to believe God. The epistle of James tells us that Abraham believed God and it was credited to him for righteousness. It also says that he was known as a friend of God. To trust God is to honour Him; to honour Him is to be His friend. Conversely, the ten spies gave an evil report to the Israelites. They incited them to rebel against the leadership and oppose God's plan to take them into the Promised Land. They exhibited a lack of faith that showed their disdain for God. In God's eyes, they were dishonouring Him.

> How long will this wicked community grumble against me? I have heard the complaints of these grumbling Israelites (Numbers 14:27).

Psalm 78 recounts the great things God did for the Israelites and their persistent refusal to trust God. Rather, they forgot His works and doubted His ability.

> They spoke against God; they said, "Can God really spread a table in the wilderness? True, he struck the rock, and water gushed out, streams flowed abundantly, but can he also give us bread? Can he supply meat for his people? (Psalm 78:19-20).

The fire of judgement broke out among them. Why?

> for they did not believe in God or trust in his deliverance (Psalm 78:22).

Then he rained down manna on them and meat like dust. The shocking thing is that the Bible says:

> In spite of all this, they kept on sinning; in spite of his wonders, they did not believe (Psalm 78:32).

Believing God is honouring God. It is saying that we think Him good and able. Understandably the Bible says that we cannot please Him without faith. We must believe when we come to Him that He rewards us for it. Constantly doubting His Word as Israel did in the above passages prohibits a friendship based on trust.

Total Surrender to Divine Purpose

One of the striking things about our father Abraham is that he completely threw his lot in with God. He did not have Plan B; his entire being was caught up in following the plan of God. There is a place of symbiosis with God in the Spirit where His desires become our desires, His plan, our plans, His heart, our heart. At that point, our lives and not just our tongues honour God. Our lips speak in harmony with our hearts, we surrender completely. Look what the Lord said about the people:

> The Lord says: 'These people come near to me with their mouth and honour me with their lips, but their hearts are far from me. Their worship of me is based on merely human rules they have been taught' (Isaiah 29:13 13).

God is looking for people who will embrace His heart and love what He loves. He wants people, like Jesus, who will do what He does, for their own selves, for the church, and for their generation.

> God is not selfish, and He is not the friend of the selfish. Unless we love what God loves and hate what God hates, we cannot be His friends[6]
> Spurgeon

Sexual purity

The Scriptures make the assertion that our bodies must honour God, which means that they must not be used for sexually immoral acts. Our bodies are not our possession. They belong to God. They are temples of the Holy Spirit whom we received from God.

> Flee from sexual immorality. All other sins a person commits are outside the body, but whoever sins sexually, sins against their own body. Do you not know that your bodies are temples of the Holy Spirit, who is in you, whom you have received from God? You are not your own; you were bought at a price. Therefore honour God with your bodies (1 Corinthians 6:18-20).

When we live in sexual purity, we are honouring God with our bodies. Purity must be seen as a means of honouring God, not as a means of avoiding hell. I pray

---

6   Spurgeon, C. H. (1969). (Friend of God). The Metropolitan Tabernacle pulpit: Sermons preached and revised in 1887. London: Banner of Truth Trust.

that you will have a greater passion to honour God than to avoid hell.

SPEAKING GOOD OF HIM; WITNESSING - OF HIS GOODNESS

How else do we honour God? We honour God by telling of His goodness, His works and His offer of salvation, by witnessing to the unsaved. The grand plan of Jesus for humanity is to rescue them from sin and reconcile them to the Father. Harmony with the Father is harmony with His purpose, that of making humans His friends. The Scriptures say that people cannot be converted unless they hear, and they cannot hear unless someone preaches.

We honour God by speaking good about Him, His works, His service; never a negative word about the things of God. The devil tries to bring sadness, discouragement, and frustration as we serve God. And it is easy to fall into the trap of thinking that life would be easier if we were not so committed to the things of God. That is an outright fallacy. It is an old lie, in fact, told from the beginning of time. In Malachi's day, some were saying this same thing and God said, 'Not so', and stated categorically that there will be a difference between those who were committed to Him and those who were not.

> "You have spoken arrogantly against me," says the LORD. "Yet you ask, 'What have we said against you?' "You have said, 'It is futile to serve God. What do we gain by carrying out his requirements and going about like mourners before the LORD Almighty? But now we call the arrogant blessed. Certainly, evildoers prosper, and even when they put God to the test, they get away with it.'" Then those who

feared the LORD talked with each other, and the LORD listened and heard. A scroll of remembrance was written in his presence concerning those who feared the LORD and honoured his name. "On the day when I act," says the LORD Almighty, "they will be my treasured possession. I will spare them, just as a father has compassion and spares his son who serves him. And you will again see the distinction between the righteous and the wicked, between those who serve God and those who do not (Malachi 3:13-18)."

Doesn't this passage make you want to shout for joy? He said 'they will be my treasured possession'. God always likes to have a special relationship with His own. That special friendship is offered to you today.

Submitting to His Word

In the previous chapter, we talked about seeking God in His Word as He is, not as we would like Him to be. Indeed, to truly walk with God, we must submit to His Word, accept it as true and choose to guide our lives by it. The psalmist cried out

> I have set your words in my heart that I may not sin against thee (Psalms 119:11).

We must set His Word in our hearts. Submitting to His Word honours Him as it entails acceptance of the superiority of His thoughts and ways over ours. When we argue with God, we put our thoughts forward as higher than His.

Blessed Life - Living the Fullness of the Covenant

We honour God by living out the fullness of the covenant. God's Word tells us that He has given us exceedingly great and precious promises. We find that in every domain of our lives God has made the provision for victorious living.

The onus is on us to choose to adopt a lifestyle of prayer, of faith, of obedience that will empower us to gain significant victories for God and live out the full blessings of God in our lives. Consequently, our light will shine before men and they will celebrate our Father who is in heaven.

And we will continue to enjoy divine friendship.

Partner with God

Brothers and sisters, if we are to be friends of God, we must be co-partners with Him. He gives over to us all that He has - and friendship with God will necessitate that we give to Him all that we have. It has been well said that if God is ours, we cannot be poor because God has all and we have all in having God. On the other hand, the work of God should not be poor if we can make it rich - and it should never be in straits if we can find supplies. If we are indeed the Lord's friends, we count His cause our cause, His work our work - and we throw all that we have into a joint-stock bank with the Great All-in-All.

Epilogue

I PRAY THAT YOU HAVE BEEN BLESSED AND challenged by this book to draw nearer to God. The success of our lives is predicated upon our intimacy with God. Do not turn your eyes to things that do not satisfy. Let your whole focus be on developing in your life those characteristics that please the heart of God. It is an amazing thing that the Most High God will relate to us in terms of friendship.

Let us grasp the extent of this great privilege and run into His arms to fellowship, run into His Word to know Him and live lives of full obedience. The benefits of obedience utterly dwarf the pleasures of rebellion. The only thing worth living for is to give pleasure to the Father and cooperate with Him for the fulfilment of His purposes.

> The benefits of obedience utterly dwarf the pleasures of rebellion.

We pray you have been blessed by this book. Please take a moment to leave a review on one of the online sites. Your review will help increase the visibility of the book so more people can be blessed. You will be contributing to getting this message out.

Do not forget to sign up for the newsletter on www.bolaoged.com.

About the Author

BOLA OGEDENGBE is a lover of God. She is an author, pastor and teacher. She is the founding pastor of ABBA HOUSE church in Paris, France and heads the prophetic ministry The Theophilus Company.

She is a former conference interpreter, speaks five languages and has travelled extensively globally. She has a heart for the nations and a passion to take the gospel to the world. Her weekly television programme Passion for God equips believers to live powerfully for God as she shares deep insights into God's Word.

She is a longstanding blogger and author of many books in English and French.
- Reborn, A New Identity
- Reborn A New Identity (30 day Workbook)
- An Eye to the Crown
- Appelez à l'Existence.
- Le Feu de Dieu (The Fire of God)

Sign up on her blogs for updates and free ebooks
English blog: www.bolaoged.com

French blog: www.oliviaoged.com

AN AMAZING LIFE

BOLA OLIVIA OGEDENGBE

AN AMAZING LIFE

www.ingramcontent.com/pod-product-compliance
Lightning Source LLC
LaVergne TN
LVHW041704060526
838201LV00043B/563